Basics of Options Trading

A Guide to Help You Understand the Key Fundamentals of Options Trading and All Essential Strategies to Become a Successful Trader

By

Benjamin T. Buffett

© Copyright 2020 by Benjamin T. Buffett

All rights reserved.

This document is geared towards providing exact and reliable information in regards to the topic and issue covered. The publication is sold with the idea that the publisher is not required to render accounting, officially permitted, or otherwise, qualified services. If advice is necessary, legal or professional, a practiced individual in the profession should be ordered.

From a Declaration of Principles which was accepted and approved equally by a Committee of the American Bar Association and a Committee of Publishers and Associations.

In no way is it legal to reproduce, duplicate, or transmit any part of this document in either electronic means or in printed format. Recording of this publication is strictly prohibited and any storage of this document is not allowed unless with written permission from the publisher. All rights reserved.

The information provided herein is stated to be truthful and consistent, in that any liability, in terms of inattention or otherwise, by any usage or abuse of any policies, processes, or directions contained within is the solitary and utter responsibility of the recipient reader. Under no circumstances will any legal responsibility or blame be held against the publisher for any reparation, damages, or monetary loss due to the information herein, either directly or indirectly.

Respective authors own all copyrights not held by the publisher.

The information herein is offered for informational purposes solely, and is universal as so. The presentation of the information is without contract or any type of guarantee assurance.

The trademarks that are used are without any consent, and the publication of the trademark is without permission or backing by the trademark owner. All trademarks and brands within this book are for clarifying purposes only and are owned by the owners themselves, not affiliated with this document.

Table of Contents

CHAPTER 1: INTRODUCTION TO OPTIONS TRADING 7
1.1 DEFINING OPTION TRADING 7
1.2 TYPES OF OPTIONS 10
1.3 TYPES OF ORDERS 16
1.4 TYPES OF SPREADS 20
1.5 TYPES OF TRADER AND TRADING STYLES 22
1.6 COMPARING OPTIONS TO OTHER FINANCIAL INSTRUMENTS 24

CHAPTER 2: BASIC OPTION TRADING STRATEGIES 27
2.1 THE LONG CALL 27
2.2 THE SHORT PUT 28
2.3 THE LONG PUT 30
2.4 THE MARRIED PUT 31
2.5 THE COVERED CALL 33

CHAPTER 3: ESSENTIAL STEPS FOR EFFECTIVE OPTIONS TRADING 39
3.1 BE AN OVERALL OPTIONS SELLER 39
3.2 MAXIMIZE THE NUMBER OF TRADES 43
3.3 SELL OPTIONS IN HIGH IV RANK SCENARIOS 47
3.4 SET AN APPROPRIATE PROBABILITY OF SUCCESS USING DELTA AS A PROXY 49
3.5 SELL OPTIONS THAT POSSESS LIQUIDITY IN THE OPTIONS MARKET 52
3.6 MANAGE WINNING TRADES 56
3.7 LIMIT POSITION SIZING/ALLOCATION 59

CHAPTER 4: GOLDEN RULES FOR TRADING SUCCESSFULLY 63
4.1 ALWAYS USE A TRADING PLAN 63
4.2 PROTECT YOUR TRADING CAPITAL 70
4.3 USE TECHNOLOGY 74
4.4 TREAT TRADING LIKE A BUSINESS 77

4.5 STUDY THE MARKETS 82
4.6 ALWAYS USE A STOP LOSS 87
4.7 DEVELOP A TRADING METHODOLOGY 91
4.8 RISK ONLY WHAT YOU CAN AFFORD... 96
4.9 KNOW WHEN TO STOP TRADING... 99
4.10 KEEP TRADING IN PERSPECTIVE 102
CHAPTER 5: TIPS TO BECOME A SUCCESSFUL TRADER 109
5.1 START WITH SUFFICIENT CAPITAL... 110
5.2 TRADING ISN'T EASY MONEY 115
5.3 BUILD YOUR OWN SUCCESS STRATEGY 119
5.4 BE VERY CAUTIOUS WITH LEVERAGE 124
5.5 DON'T BECOME EMOTIONALLY ATTACHED 130
5.6 LEARN ALL ABOUT RISK MANAGEMENT 135
CONCLUSION.. 141

Chapter 1: Introduction to Options Trading

Options are financial instruments whose value comes from the underlying (included) property value, such as security or stock. An option contract provides the buyer with the asset to buy or sell based on the value of the guard. The ownership of the call option allows the buyer to purchase the shares at a strike price and the property of the put option gives them the right to sell at the same value.

When buying or selling, there is no need to exercise the right only at the deadline and strike price. They can be practiced at any time until the option is exhausted. Therefore, options are considered less risky than stocks or future contracts. Thanks to this system, they are treated as derivative securities – meaning that their value depends upon the assets involved, and its price. Options, however, do not imply ownership in the company.

1.1 Defining Option Trading

When some people think about investing, they think about buying stocks in the stock market, and most of them are completely unaware of terms such as options trading.

Buying and holding shares are one of the most common investment strategies to build up a long-term return. It's best to self-invest if you have some idea of which stocks you should buy, otherwise, use a broker to give you advice and guidance on such matters.

The approach known as buy-and-hold strategy can help you increase your wealth in the long run, but it does not offer anything in the short-term. Nowadays, many investors are looking for a more active investment style to get the most immediate profit.

Thanks to many online brokers, that allow investors to trade in stock exchanges with just some clicks of their mouse, it is much simpler for them to be more active. Some people do business online on a part-time or full-time basis; trying to buy and sell regularly in order to take advantage of short-term fluctuations and, often, hold their purchases for just a few weeks or even days and sometimes hours.

Many financial tools can actively trade. Options are becoming increasingly popular, especially among traders, and options trading is becoming even more common. Options trading is similar to buying and selling options contracts and to stock trading on public exchanges.

While stock traders aim to make a profit by buying stocks and selling them at higher prices, options traders can do the same with options contracts, as stock traders take a lower position on the stock, believing that prices will fall.

In practice, however, this type of trading is far more versatile than stock trading especially for one thing; option contracts depend on a wide variety of securities, which means how to invest and make decisions. Traders can use options to bet on the price oscillation of individual stocks, indexes, foreign currencies and other commodities, providing a large number of opportunities for potential gains.

The real versatility, however, is one of the many options that can be traded and the range of different orders that can be placed.

When trading stocks, you have two main ways to make money: by taking a long position or a short position on a particular stock. If you expect an increase in the value of a specific stock, you can take a significant place by buying it to then sell it at a higher price. If you expect a particular stock price to fall, you accept the short position by selling that stock at a lower price and then repurchasing it at an even lower price. In options trading, instead, there are many ways to trade and make money.

It should be clear that trading options are more complicated than stock trading, and the whole concept of participation may seem challenging for beginners. There are little things you need to learn before you start investing your money. However, it is not so hard to understand the very basics. Once you comprehend them, it will be much easier to realise what options trading is actually.

1.2 Types of Options

There are many types of options that can be traded and categorized in many ways, but two are the main one: call and put.

Calls give the shopper the right to buy the underlying asset, with the put the buyer reserves the right to sell the underlying asset. With this apparent difference, the options are usually classified based on American or European style.

It has nothing to do with geographical location, but it's about when using contracts.

The options are then categorized by the way they are traded, their expiration cycle and their underlying security. There are also other specific types and many other overseas options.

Call options are contracts that give the owner the right to purchase the underlying asset at a future agreed price. If you believe that the cost of the underlying asset is likely to rise over a certain period, you buy the call. Calls have a termination date, and, depending on the terms of the agreement, the underlying asset may be purchased at any time, before the due date or the expiry date.

Put options are, basically, the opposite of calls. Put's owner has the right to sell the underlying asset at a predetermined price in the future. Therefore, if you are concerned that the underlying asset is depreciating, you will buy. Like the call, the contract has an expiration date.

The term "**American Style**" rights do not apply to the selling or purchasing of a contract but to the terms of the agreement. Options contracts come with an expiration date, during which the owner has the right to buy or sell the underlying security (if called). With American Style Options, the contract owner also has the right to exercise before the due date. This added flexibility is a positive advantage for the owner of the American style contract.

Holders of "**European style**" options contracts don't have the same flexibility that American style contracts holders have.

If you have a European-style deal, the contract is based only on the expiration date and not before; you have the right to buy or sell the underlying asset.

Listed options are the most common one. The term "traded" is used to describe any option agreement listed on the public trading exchange. Anyone can buy and sell them using the appropriate broker services.

Over-the-Counter (OTC) options are only traded in OTC markets, making them less accessible to the general public. They create customized contracts with more complicated terms than exchange-traded contracts.

When people refer to stock options in general, they use the term 'option' referring to the underlying asset share of a listed company. While these are, indeed, common, many other types of built-in security are a different matter.

Stock Options: The underlying asset of these agreements is exclusively in listed company shares.

Index Options: This is similar to stock options, but gives the holders the right to buy or sell the value of an underlying index, such as the S&P 500 Index.

Foreign Currency / Currency Option: This type of contract gives the owner the right to buy or sell a particular currency at an agreed exchange rate.

Futures options: This type of implied security is a specified forward contract. The futures option essentially gives the owner the right to enter into a specified futures contract.

Commodity Choices: The underlying asset of this type of contract may be a physical or a futures contract.

Contracts are classified by their closing cycle, which requires the owner to exercise his/her right to buy or sell the relevant property under the terms of the contract.

Some deals are only available with a specific type of closing cycle, in others you can choose. For most option traders, this information is not necessary, but it can help identify situations. Below are some details on different contract types, based on their closing cycle.

Regular Options: These are based on the standard expiration cycles listed under the option contract. When purchasing this type of deal, you have at least four different deadline months to choose from. Expiration cycles are a bit complicated, but you need to understand that you can choose your ideal expiration date from at least four different months of choice.

Weekly Options: Also known as the end of the week, they were introduced in 2005. They are currently available in a limited number of securities, including some key indicators, but their popularity is exponentially growing. The critical principle of weeklies is the same as that of regular options, but they have a much shorter expiration period.

Quarterly options: Quarterly, they classified for exchanges with the closest four quarters expiry and the last quarter of the following year.

Unlike ordinary contracts, which expire on the third Friday of the month, the quarter ends on the last day of the month.

Long-Term Securities: These long-term contracts are commonly known as LEAPS; they are available in a wide range of underlying securities. LEAPS always terminate in January but can be purchased with due dates for the next three years.

It is a form of stock option where employees are given contracts based on the company's stock. They are usually used as a remuneration, bonus or incentive to join an organization.

There is no physical transfer of the underlying asset when exercising or landing the CAS settlement agreements. Instead, the other party pays in cash in the form of which party gains on the contract.

These types of arrangements are usually used when the underlying asset is difficult or expensive to transfer to another party.

A different option is a term applied to a contract with more complex conditions. They also classified as non-standard alternatives. There are a lot of various international agreements, anyway, most of them are only available from OTC markets.

However, some foreign contracts are more popular with mainstream investors and they are listed on public exchanges. A few more common types are listed below.

Barrier options: They offer payment to the contract holder if the underlying security (or contractual terms) reaches a predetermined price.

Binary Options: When this type of contract ends, they're offered a set sum of money for a profit to the consumer.

Selector Options: These are named "selectors" because they allow the contract owner to choose whether to call or put when there is a specific date.

Compound options: These are options where the underlying security is another option contract.

Look Back Option: This type of contract does not have strike value but, instead, allows the employer to exercise at the best price, until reaching the underlying security, for the duration of the contract.

1.3 Types of Orders

The primary common types of orders are:

- market orders
- limit orders
- stop-loss orders.

Market order: you can buy or sell a security. It guarantees that the law is executed, but does not guarantee the execution value. A market order usually runs a price near the current bid, or asks for a quotation for a sale or a buy order.

However, investors should remember that the last traded price is not necessarily the price to execute the market order.

Restriction order: you can buy or sell good security at, or above, a specific price. They can only perform at the order limit price, or lower, and the sales limit will only apply at the order limit, or higher. Example: An investor does not want to buy shares of ABC stock for more than $ 10.

The investor can submit a restriction order for this amount, and this order will only take place if the ABC stock price is $ 10 or less.

Buy Stop order: also called a **stop-loss order**; you can buy or sell the stock after that its price reaches a certain amount, known as the stop price. When the stop price is touched, it becomes a market order.

Sell stop order: it takes place with a higher price than the current market price. Investors, usually, use sell-stop rules to limit losses, or protect profits, on their stock. You can also add time parameters to your order using the timestamp. The following timing orders are the most commonly used; they provide specific instructions to your broker about situations in which the law has to be filled, or cancelled.

AON - All or none. is a directive, used on a buy or sell order, to fill the order completely or not at all. E.g., if you are trying to purchase a contract of 100 options at a given price, but your broker will buy only 90 at that price, the order will not fill.

All or none orders are open until they are fully executed; It does not automatically expire even though it cancelled.

Day Order: it is an options order that must fill in on a particular trading day. If it cannot fill before the day's market closes, it will be automatically cancelled.

FOK - Fill or Kill: it is very similar to the AON, however, if the option order cannot be filled immediately, it is automatically cancelled.

GTC - Good to Cancel: this type of order is open until it filled, or you decide to cancel it. It does not expire until you manually cancel it.

IOC - Instant or Cancellation: this option is similar to the fill or kill order but with a significant difference, this type of option order can be partially filled out and it will automatically cancel out the rest.

MOC – Market on Close: it is a non-limit order and it can take place after, or at, a closing a stock exchange. They are executed as closer as possible at the closing price.

Trailing Stop Order: This is the option to specify a stop price based on the change from the best price. That change can express as a whole number or percentage.

For example, if the option falls below 5% of its highest rate, a trailing stop order can be set to close a location.

Contingency Commands: These order commands are straightforward and can be used to exit an open position based on the criteria you choose. For example, you can use contingency to sell the stock option if you contract, so the underlying stock price, increases by a certain percentage.

Combination orders: used in many basic and advanced options trading strategies, combination orders refer to the name: they are commands that combine two different orders to coordinate the entry, and departure, of multiple locations in the selection contracts.

OTO - One Triggers the Other: This type of selection combination sequence means that the secondary selection sequence is activated automatically when the primary one is filled. It is the most common form of combination order used in options trading.

OCO – One Cancels the Other: This combination order means that one of them is cancelled when another request is filled.

1.4 Types of Spreads

The real benefit of options trading comes from using their spreads. It is entirely possible to make profits, in any market situation, using a combination of direct buying and selling of calls and putts. Still, if you learn to use the option spread, you will find many more opportunities to make a profit.

The spread has a position on the agreement of two, or more, different options based on the same underlying security.

For example, if you buy a deal on a particular stock and write an agreement on the equal share, you must make the spread option.

It is mainly used for two specific reasons: limiting risk and reducing the upfront cost of taking a particular position. However, there are many different varieties, and some of them are very simple, others very complex.

The simplest way to categorize a spread is to use basic options: call or put. Although some spreads can use a combination of both, most of them are just used as call or put. A call spread refers to buying a call on a strike and selling another one on a higher strike of the same expiry.

A put spread, instead, refers to buying a put on a strike and selling another put on a lower one of the same expiry.

Threads can be easily categorized based on the cost of capital involved. When you create one, you take advantage of the upfront cost, or receive an upfront credit. Taking advantage of the upfront cost, by paying more than buying contracts obtained from contract writing, is called a debit spread. Getting advanced credit by spending less on contracts, it's called a credit spread.

Vertical spreads: this is another way of classifying spreads based on the relative position of each other in an options series. Ranges with the same purchase and write-offs, the same expiration date, and the same underlying security appear to be stacked vertically on a selection chain with different strike prices, that's the why of their name.

Horizontal spreads: buying and writing contracts with different due dates but with the same strike price and the same underlying security. Buy and sell options have different strike prices and expiration dates, but they have the same underlying security, which creates a diagonal spread.

These options have different expiration dates. Horizontal and diagonal spreads are examples of a calendar spread, but there are other types. They must be used to benefit from a variety of depreciation rates between written contracts and acquired contracts.

It applies to any spread, such as buying and selling a variety of option contracts, in contrast to purchasing a contract amount equal to the written amount. They usually write more deals than they buy, but the ratio works anyway regardless the strategy used.

1.5 Types of Trader and Trading Styles

While the basics of options trading are not very difficult, you need to be very informed before you can feel comfortable getting started. The fundamentals are simple; you need to understand what is involved, what the benefits are, what the risks are, and how the options work.

We'll cover these unique items, and more, in our introduction about Options Trading, but there are many other things you need to know if you want to have an excellent chance to make money.

One significant example could be the use of different types of trading styles, which can be used with various options traders.

Generally, brokers can be divided into two categories. First, you have the experts, who usually work for large financial institutions, directly on behalf of those companies or clients. They can also fill the role of professional market makers.

Second, you have private individuals who can undoubtedly do business on their behalf using their capital, and they usually do business from home. Some of them trade full-time, making their profits as their primary source of income, while others trade on a part-time basis.

It is a full-time style to use other financial instruments such as trading options or stocks. This is usually preferred by professionals, but, in the last few years, it has also been widely used by private individuals. It is an intensive and time-consuming activity that requires constant monitoring of daytime markets, properly named since it contains transactions that do not last longer than one day (meaning you close all positions at the end of the day to realize any gains and take effect the next day).

Another style, called **swing trading** (the idea is basically to detect and benefit from price changes and to buy and sell appropriately), is used to trade multiple financial instruments along with options. It is one of the most recognized forms of trading and can be used by any investor or trader.

It is suitable for part-time traders who are unable to dedicate many hours of their day to this business and are not ready for the intensity of day trading.

It is the most used style for trading options and futures, has a relatively low-risk but requires a comprehensive understanding of the mechanics of the options and their business. It is not a style that beginners should consider and is mainly used by professionals who have the experience and information necessary to succeed.

Market makers are well-known experts in option exchanges. They guarantee that every time there is enough depth and liquidity in the market, so that traders can execute the transactions they want. Market makers buy and sell large volumes, and traders facilitate transactions if there is no relevant buyer or seller in the market.

It helps to ensure market movements effectively. They usually are employees of financial institutions.

1.6 Comparing Options to Other Financial Instruments

When it comes to general trade and investment, a variety of financial instruments are used for potential gains; a financial instrument is essentially any traditional asset. Whether it is cash, proof of ownership in a company, a contractual right to receive or distribute other goods or any other financial instrument.

Stocks are probably the most known financial instruments, but there are also bonds, futures and, of course, options contracts. If you know what you are doing, investing, or trading, in any financial instrument will let you make money.

If you are interested in options trading, you should know what the options are and how they work. However, it also works to understand and pay for other financial instruments. If there are only trading options in your investment plan, it can help you learn a little more about other financial instruments.

If you are wondering how people want to start investing, the most common answer is: by buying stocks at locally listed companies. That's because buying shares is the simplest way to spend money, and anyone can do it with less knowledge.

However, there are some distinct advantages that options offer when comparing trading stocks to trading options.

Bonds are another direct way to invest, and they particularly attract risk-averse investors who prefer traditional, safe investments. Securities as options are a form of a two-party financial arrangement, but bonds and options vary from one another.

Forex trading in about foreign currencies and has gained considerable popularity in recent years. Successful forex traders can create a great source of income through this technique. However, it requires a lot of time and effort and is a stressful and critical way to invest.

Forex is one of the many financial instruments that create the underlying security of options contracts, so it is possible to trade and speculate the currencies simultaneously.

However, options contracts are not the same as foreign currencies and financial instruments.

Futures and options are two financial instruments mostly used by investors and traders, often for similar reasons. There are many similarities between the two types of agreements, and, often, they are confused with each other. However, there is a primary difference between the two.

Usually, financial instruments are totally different from each other, but most are very similar. Warrants and options are two financial instruments identical in many aspects, tht's why many investors and traders believe they are the same thing. While they share many features, there are some essential differences between the two.

Chapter 2: Basic Option Trading Strategies

Option trading strategies range from simple levels to very complex ones. But easy or difficult, they all use the same approach, based on two basic choices: call and put.

Below are five common option strategies to start with: investors can call one-legged the ones where only one option is traded. Simple doesn't mean risk-free, but these are some excellent ways to get started with options trading.

2.1 The Long Call

Long calls are a strategy where you buy call options that "last longer." The strategy is that the underlying stock will rise above the strike price rather than the closing price.

Example: XYZ stock trades at $ 50 per share, and the call of 50 strikes is $ 5 with a deadline of six months. The contract costs 100 shares, and this call costs $ 500: $ 5 premium x 100..

Potential Downside: If the call is well-timed, the long call is theoretically infinite, as long as it is high.

If the stock moves incorrectly, traders can often save some premium by selling the call before it expires. The downside is the complete loss of premium payments, - $ 500 in this example.

Why use it: If you're not worried about losing the entire premium, a long call is one way to place a bet on the stock and make a lot more profit than owning the stock directly. It is one way to limit the risk of directly owning it. For example, some traders may use a higher call instead of having a comparable number of shares, which will turn them upside down, but the cost of the call limits their trouble; owning the stock, and the high price - they may fall in the interim.

2.2 The Short Put

A short put is the opposite of the long one, in which the investor sells the put or "goes short." This strategy implies that the stock will remain flat or will continue to expire, than the put expires, and the put seller moves at a full premium. Like a long call, short put maybe a bet on stock growth, but with notable differences.

Example: XYZ sells in stock at $50 per share, and a $ 50 strike can sell for $ 5 with a deadline of six months. In total, the put is sold for $ 500: $ 5 premium x 100 shares. The payment profile of the shot put is the opposite of the long put.

Potential Reverse / Downside: While a long call bets on a significant increase in the stock, the short put is a humbler, smaller bet. A long call can return the coefficients of the original investment; the maximum return premium for a short put, of $ 500, which the seller receives in advance.

If the stock is above the strike price, the seller charges a full premium. If the stock is beneath the strike price, at the time of expiration, the putt seller may be required to purchase the capital during the strike after the loss realized. The maximum fall is when the stock is trading at $ 0 per share. In that case, the short-put strike cost x 100 x the number of contracts, or lose $ 5,000.

Why use it: Investors often use small putts to generate income, selling premiums to other investors and betting that the stock will fall. Sellers should aim to sell premiums and not pay it back.

However, investors must sell those parts, because they are on the hook to buy shares if the stock expires less than the strike. A falling stock can swiftly eat up any premiums on a putt.

Sometimes investors use a small put to bet on stock appreciation, especially when the business does not require immediate expense. But, unlike a long call, the strategy can be overshadowed and with a more significant downside, if the stock falls.

Investors use a short put to get a reasonable buy price on meagre stocks and sell a putt at a slim strike price, where they prefer to buy shares. For example, at $ 50 with XYZ stock, the investor can sell put 2 with 40 strike prices, then:

If the stock is less than a strike by the expiration date, the put vendor assigned to the capital with the premium paid to offset the purchase price. The investor already pays a strike price of $ 38 per share or $ 2 premium minus $ 40 per share.

If the stock exceeds the strike by the time it expires, the put seller has the cash and can retry the strategy.

2.3 The Long Put

Long put is the same as a long call; you are spinning when the stock is not decreasing. The investor buys the put option, betting that the stock will expire over time.

Example: XYZ stock trades at $ 50 per share, and the six 50 strike puts it at $ 5 with a deadline of six months. In total, the put price is $ 500: $ 5 premium x 100 shares. Here is a lengthy contract payment profile.

Potential Reverse / Negative: Long put price is highest when the stock is at $ 0 per share, so its maximum value is the strike price x 100 x number of contracts. In this example, it's $ 5,000. If the stock goes up, traders can still sell the putt and save some premiums as long as the deadline is up — full loss of maximum fall premium or $ 500 here.

Why it should be used: If you can survive the potential loss of the entire premium, a long stack is one way to place a bet on stock depreciation. If the stock goes down significantly, traders will earn more by selling the stock for less. Some traders may use more time to limit their potential losses compared to short-selling, where the risk is not reduced since, in theory, the stock price may go up indefinitely, and the stock will not expire.

2.4 The Married Put

A married put is a strategy for options where the investor buys the equivalent of the underlying stock and the "least-money" option.

Married puts are an effective strategy to protect against stock price depreciation. From this book, investors will learn the basics of the married put, and that it is best to use this strategy in their own options trading playbook.

It is used when the investor is bullish on the stock, but there are some uncertainties about the stock shortly.

Married puts owner has unlimited profit potential because there is no limit to appreciating the underlying stock price. However, the opportunity cost of using this strategy is lower than owning the stock. It is due to the premium paid when buying the put option.

An investor applies a premium cost to protect his stock from adverse risk. This strategy is called a capital protection strategy and not a profit-making approach.

Let us look at an example to better understand this strategy. Suppose ABC is trading at $ 100. An investor holds a married position by buying ABC shares for $ 100, while a put option at a strike price of $ 97 ends in a month. He buys the put option at $ 3 per share.

The buyer's maximum loss is when the stock drops to $ 97 or less by the time it expires. Suppose ABC dropped to $ 90. With the put option, the buyer can sell shares of stock for $ 97. His maximum loss is, therefore, $6.00 per share, which calculates a stock's selling price from $100 to $97, which is a loss of $3 and costs $3 of the premium paid. If the stock price expires at $ 100 at the settled time, the buyer will only lose the premium cost, which is $ 3 per share.

Buyer's Maximum Profit: ABC increased to $ 105 by the end of the year. The buyer will have a profit (from $ 100 to $ 105 stock price). After calculating the put option's price, that was $ 3 per share, the buyer's total profit will be $ 2 per share. Suppose ABC went for $ 130 at the expiration date. The buyer would get $ 30 profit from the original stock price ($ 100). Subtracting the put option cost (3$), the total profit of the buyer would be $ 27 per share. It shows how the buyer's potential benefit is set aside and can keep up with the rise in stock prices.

From these scenarios, shareholders should have a better understanding of the married put strategy. It is an excellent strategy to use when an investor wants to limit their risks but, on the other hand, has limited potential.

2.5 The Covered Call

A covered call refers to a transaction in the financial market in which an investor, who sells a call option, has an equal amount of underlying security. To run with a long position in an asset, an investor writes the call (sell) option on the same property to create an income stream. An investor's long situation in the park is "covered" because the buyer of the call option can distribute the seller's shares if they choose to exercise. If an investor buys a stock and, at same time, writes a call option against that stock's position, it is called a "buy-write" transaction.

Covered Call is a neutral strategy, meaning that the investor can expect only a slight increase, or reduction, in the underlying stock price for the life of the written call option. This strategy is often used when the investor has a short-term neutral view of the property, and for this reason, the asset is long-term and short-lived by the option of earning income from the option premium.

If an investor wants to keep the underlying stock for a long time, but does not expect significant price increases in the near term, they can earn an income (premium) for their account while they wait for Lula. The cover call works as a short-term hedge in the case of long-term stock and allows investors to earn income through the deductible premiums received for written options. However, the investor gets the stock if the price is higher than the strike price of the opportunity. If the buyer chooses, they will be responsible for providing 100 shares at the strike price (per contract). The cover call strategy is neither too fast nor too helpful for most investors. If the investor has no patient, they are usually better off not writing options and owning stocks. This option increases the profit on the capital, which reduces the overall profitability of the business when the share price goes up. Similarly, if an investor is very bearish, they may be better off selling the stock, because the premium received by the call option write-off does little to reduce the loss on the stock.

The maximum benefit of a cover call is equal to the strike price of the short call option, the purchase price of the underlying stock, and the premium received. The maximum loss is equal to the purchase price of the underlying stock, which is less than the premium received.

Let's have a look at an example:

An investor owns shares of an imaginary company, TSJ. They are attracted by its long-term prospects, as well as its share price, but feel that in the short term the stock will likely stay quite flat: possibly within a couple dollars of its recent price of $25.

If they sell the call option on TSJ with a strike price of $27, they earn the premium from the option sale but, for the length of the option, cap their upside on the stock to $27. Let's assume that the premium they receive for writing a three-month call option is $0.75 ($75 per contract or 100 shares).

One of two pictures will play out:

- TSJ shares trade below the $27 strike price. The option will expire valueless and the investor will keep the premium from the option. In this case, by using the buy-write strategy they have successfully outperformed the stock.

They still own the stock plus, they have an extra $75 in their pocket, less fees.

- TSJ shares rise above $27. The option is exercised, and the upside in the stock is capped at $27. If the price rise above $27.75, the investor would have been better off holding the stock. Although, if they planned to sell at $27, no matter what, writing the call option gave them an additional $0.75 per shares.

The buyer pays a premium to the seller of the call option to obtain the right to buy shares, or contracts, at a future price. Premium cash charge the day the choice is sold, and the seller keeps the money, regardless of whether the option exercised or not. If the capital moves up to the strike price and generates a profit from a long stock position, the cover call is more profitable. Still, the sold Call ends up being useless, allowing the call writer to collect the whole premium from their sales.

When you sell a covered call, you get paid in exchange for giving up a portion of future benefit. For instance, let's assume you buy ZXY stock for $50 per share, supposing it will rise to $60 in one year. You're also willing to sell at $55 within the next 6 months, giving up further profit, but taking a short-term profit. With this picture, selling a covered call on the position might be an attractive strategy.

The stock's option chain shows that selling a $55 six-month call option will cost the buyer a $4 per share premium. You can sell the option in opposition to your shares, which you purchased at $50 and hope to sell at $60 within a year. Writing this covered call generates an obligation to sell the shares at $55 within six months, if the underlying price reaches that level.

You get to keep the $4 in premium plus the $55 from the share sale, for a total of $59 (or an 18%) return over six months.

Instead, you'll suffer a $10 loss on the original position if the stock falls to $40. However, you get to keep the $4 premium from the call option sale, reducing the total loss from $10 to $6 per share.

Selling cover call options can reduce the risk, or add an upside-down, taking a cash premium for the future beyond the contract's term. In other words, if ZXY stock closes above $ 59, for example, the seller makes less money than if he owned the stock. However, if the stock goes below $ 59 per share within six months, the seller makes more money, or loses less money, than if the option did not sell.

Call sellers must hold underlying shares, or contracts, they may hold, also, naked calls, which could theoretically cause immense risks if the underlying security increased.

Therefore, if sellers want to sell shares or contracts, they must repurchase option positions before the deadline, reducing than the net profit, or lower net losses, while increasing transaction costs. Using a cover call to reduce the cost base or benefit from shares and futures contracts adds a profit generator to stock or contract ownership.

Like any strategy, writing a cover call has its advantages and disadvantages. When used with the correct stock, covered calls can be a perfect way to reduce losses, or produce income, from your daily costs.

Chapter 3: Essential Steps for Effective Options Trading

3.1 Be an Overall Options Seller

Generally, you want to be an option seller because, in the process, you are not looking at how the market will grow and still collecting premium income. Stocks can trade up and down, and you can make money by the time they expire because you are using time decay to your advantage. Time always passes, and as the option expires the premium becomes a real gain, since the premium declines at all times until the stock breaks through the strike price.

In the world of buying and selling stock options, the last one is the best strategy when considering trading. Bullish investors may purchase a call or sell a put; if things don't go as expected, they can buy a put or sell a call.

There are many alternatives to choose from and each of them has different strategies, one of them is called "selling the option." This strategy explains why the options are favourable to the seller, how to gain the possibility of success in selling an opportunity and the risks associated with trading the options.

The call option gives the call buyer the right to buy the underlying capital at the strike price of the option, in a specific period; keep in mind that is not an obligation. The strike price is the value that converts the option contract into security shares. The put option qualifies the buyer of the opportunity but is not responsible for selling the stock at the option's strike price. Each option has a due date or expiration.

Many elements are included in the value of the option contract and if it will be profitable until the end of the contract. This option compares the strike price and the remaining time with the current price of the stock; this plays a vital role in determining the value of your choice.

The value of an option is made up of intrinsic and time value. The inherent value is the difference between the original value strike price and the stock price in the market and depends on the activity of the stock.

If an option is an ITM ("in the money") it means that its current stock price has surpassed its strike price; its intrinsic value is more significant.

An "out of the money" (OTM) option, means that it has a strike price hasn't reach yet the underlying security; its inherent value is null. OTM option contracts have a lower premium.

The option premium is the upfront fee charged by the option buyer. The option with a high intrinsic value option has a higher premium than the null intrinsic value option.

In options trading, time value refers to the portion of an option's price that is attributable to the amount of time remaining until the expiration of the option contract. The premium of any option consists of two components: its intrinsic value and its time value; the total premium of an option is equal to the intrinsic value plus the option's time value.

The more time the option remains without expiration date, the greater the time value of it will be; in general, an option loses one-third of its time value during the first half of its life, and the remaining two-thirds during the second half.

So, the time value decreases over time at an accelerating pace, this phenomenon is known as time decay/time-value decay.

The process of declining the premium of an option can be worth it. Depreciation means the premium value of the option is decreasing over time. As time passes, the decay of time approaches.

High premium options are a benefit for sellers. However, once the option vendor starts trading, and pays the premium, they usually want to be as useless as pocketing the premium.

In other terms, the contract seller, typically, doesn't want to use or revoke the right. Instead, they want the income from the right without getting the duty to sell or purchase the underlying securities.

As the time pass, moving closer to the maturity the expiration date, the option will lose value. Theta is the name of the measure that rate this decline in value.

Generally, theta, is a negative number that can be seen as the amount of the value decline that the option will get every day.

Selling options is a positive theta trade, which means that as time goes on, the situation will make more money.
During an option transaction, the buyer expects the stock to move in one direction supposing to have a profit from it.

Option values are made of both extrinsic and intrinsic value (if applicable). When the option expires, all that remains is the intrinsic value, if any, since time is an important part of the extrinsic value.

Option writers are the main beneficiaries of the devaluation of an option's value, since it will be cheaper for them to buy options back to close out short positions.

Remember, a premium is paid to the optional vendor before they can start trading. As a result, option sellers are the beneficiaries of the contract value. When the option's premium is reduced, the seller of the option may close its position with the offset trade by repurchasing the option at a lower premium.

3.2 Maximize the Number of Trades

It is a need to maximize the number of trades in order to give more shots to the target and have more opportunities through all market conditions. If you set your success chances at 85%, you get an 85%-win rate in the long run, which will give you enough business occasions. If you only have ten trades, you are unlikely to win 8, but if you do have 100 trades, or 1,000 trades, your chances will increase.

Long call option strategy is riskier than most traders realize. Average, three of the options placed result being useless, so, you need to become an expert in time to improve those odds. In a swing trading strategy, extended options reduce the risk of stacking and stretching. You can use long puts at the top of the swing and long calls at the bottom, which significantly reduces your market risk. Since time-lapse is no longer a factor, options that end within a month provide the best benefit.

Short term for high annual returns: when you write a cover call, long-term contracts may get more cash, but, every year, your yield is always higher when writing short-term contracts. To make an annual yield, divide the premium by strike; then divide by the holding period; then multiply by 12.

Spreads straddle and synthetics during exceptionally high volatility: whenever you open spreads, straddles, or synthetic stock positions, you can add open short option locations. Because of the more rapid decline at the end of the option's life, when you use more concise duration expressions, you get higher annual returns, especially if you see a spike in volatility. It is a brief-term, so when the premium is expensive, the option premium changes quickly.

Remember, time decay is a big problem for long option locations, so it's a significant advantage when you stay short.

It is the essence of efficiency—lower efforts to achieve better results (excellent quality). However, you have to be very careful and don't confuse laziness for efficiency. The lower the number of transactions, the higher the effort required to manufacture. Do less business but more research. Don't try to use every trick, and most importantly, don't kick yourself for not doing business. It is one of the most significant downsides when weak traders get upset for a trade they don't take.

It is a sign of complete waste of time and weakness. Focus on improving efficiency by making choices in transactions.

Including a solid watch list of shares that can trade on a solid morning preparation routine, every percentage of the watch list should have trends, support/resistance price levels, possible sample setup and be ready. Having this information upfront, will put you ahead of most traders. Please pay attention to your watchlist's stocks so that you don't have to focus too much on it.

Removing 20 stocks on a watch list is easy. The important thing is only to filter and filter potential candidates. Having less capital to monitor means more focus. Keep an active watch list and regularly check it.

Active Watch List is accompanied by Stock to Trade that day. When the activity has dried up, they may move to the general watch list, but it could still be worth watching for potential setups. The active watch list demands urgent attention as viable stocks in the public watch list require time to shape trend setups. The trick is to limit your concentration, and not to water down your efforts. One trade that generates a profit of $1000 is more efficient than ten businesses, making a profit of $100 each.

Technical indicators are useful in detect patterns and triggers, and most of them can backfire. Try to minimize your technical indicators so that they give the appropriate indication.

For example, when a single-speed indicator such as RSI and MACD exceeds the randomness in the chart, overkill. Too many indicators can lead to difficult decision and have a foggy mind. Be frugal and choose only the most accurate indicators to track price action, momentum and targets. Remember that every indicator will help you in the other decision-making process of the business.

If your indicators cover your chart, the candles are no longer visible, which means you have too many signs.

Every business person has power. Unfortunately, his weaknesses outweigh him at the worst time. It is essential to cry for the strength you have as an entrepreneur. Analyse your best trades to see what worked and what was your mentality. When it comes to determining strength, be objective.

Are you a stable scalar or swing trader? Do you prefer short-selling or long-term buying? Do you desire to get out of the office quickly, or do you want to manage positions? How do you respond to a losing situation? Do you have the discipline to wait for the trigger, before returning? Do you have control and determination? How many losing trades do you take before doubling in size? Which model do you have the most success with? With these questions, you can increase your strength.

If you are successful with short-selling stocks, commit to short sales, and reduce long-term trades. Are you having more success with shares of $ 20 or more? The goal here is to lower the standards to map your business personality.

For example, you could be a scalar, which works best in the first hour of the trading day in a descending triangle pattern of short-stacking stocks at $ 20. From there, you specialize in meeting those standards with your trades and measuring when they trigger. Always make sure you are in your comfort zone when doing business.

3.3 Sell Options in High IV Rank Scenarios

Selling options in high IV rank scenarios; ideal because it is full of yield options, so there is a significant premium. The key to success in options trading is the implied volatility and its rank. Since the implied volatility mainly determines the option premium price, it is the inherent volatility component that gives the option traders the edge, when used appropriately. When IV increases, options increase as well in value, and when IV decreases, options go the same way. Historically, this volatility has always been used to reduce real volatility and to benefit sellers. Therefore, the number of options contracts represents the real stock movement.

This overstimulation is an option where traders can sell more options to make a profit, and have a chance of success. The IV rank is a measure of the current implied volatility against the historical suggested volatility range (IV low - IV high) over one year.

Option sellers can pay high premiums with the expectation that volatility will return to its meaning. The higher the IV rank the richer the bonus, and when the options life cycle unfolds and this volatility decreases, the option time value decreases, also the option price decreases, so that lifetime benefits has to be realized in advance without waiting for the contract to expire. Possible.

Relative volatility is useful for comparing apples with apples in the options market. Relative volatility refers to the volatility of a stock compared to the volatility of time. Suppose stock A's money options expiring in one month have inherent fluctuations of 10%, but now showing 20% IV, stock B's one-month money option has historically held 30% of IV, which has now increased by 35%. On a relative basis, it is clear that stock B has made a significant change in relative volatility, even though stock B has absolute volatility. The overall level of broad market volatility is also an important factor when assessing individual stocks. The best-called measure of market volatility is the CBOE Volatility Index (VIX), which measures the S&P 500.

Also called the Fear Gauge, when the S&P 500 drops significantly, the VIX accelerates; opposite to that, when the S&P 500 goes smoothly, the VIX increase again.

The basic principle of investment is buying at low price and selling at higher one, and trading options is no different. Therefore, options traders usually sell (or write) options when volatility is high. Likewise, when the implied volatility is low, the options trader buys the option or "long period" at the volatility.

In the Iron Condor Strategy, the trader spreads a bear's call with the same time-limited bull, hoping to recover through volatility, causing stocks to fall within the life of trading options.

In general, the difference between call and put's strike is the same: intrinsic.

3.4 Set an Appropriate Probability of Success Using Delta as a Proxy

Determine your chances of success: if you want to win 70%, 80% or 90% of your trades, determine your likelihood of success with long-term options. There is no edge in stock picking; the stock is a binary phenomenon and boiled down to a 50:50 probability. In options, we can determine the likelihood of success in our favour and sales options, and combine higher IV ranks; this setup allows us to pay significant premiums with a high probability of success.

Let's have a look at Facebook as an example, at $178 per share and one-month trading in the future, we can see that 85% of the stock does not trade below the $ 160 strike price, thus capturing the benefits of premium allowance.

Technically, the value of the Delta of the option is the first derivative of the value of the option, relative to the price of the underlying security. Delta shows how changes in underlying rates affect option contract pricing.

For example, suppose an investor has a call option with a delta of $ -0.30 we mention to this as a 30-delta call, with no decimal or symbol. If the underlying capital increases by $ 1, the option price will theoretically decrease by 30 cents and vice versa. But there are more practical applications in Delta.

Delta is commonly used by merchants as money (as percentage). Its values are not equal to the actual percentage currency, but in practical cases, they are very close.

For example, if the deadline is today, and the option contract makes money, it will be in the capital (e.g., 84 deltas), but if payment not paid it is said to be out of money (16 deltas), and if the current price and strike price are the same, it will be on the money (50 deltas) Is said to be. If you are a short seller, the opposite is exact; 16 Delta Short puts are OTM and profitable.

We use Delta to call our strategies for support. There are many benefits to doing this.

By using the first Delta, you are defining a position independent of the underlying price values normalized. We may, therefore, have continuity between the different periods and underlying it.

30 Delta Short Stringer, for example, is the same strategy, whether the stock is at $ 100 or $ 200. You should equate the 2012 strategy outcomes where the stock is at $40 with a 2018 proposal, where the money is at $120. In this example, it has put and call sales equal to a standard deviation at 16 deltas. Delta Neutral Strategy.

Due to the half standard deviation, if we use the 30 Delta option on the PUT side, the result is a more rapid strategy:

Sell PUT, which is 0.5% OTM. Depending on the volatility of the underlying PUT, there may be very different possibilities for success. The curve denotes stocks with high volatility. A small PUT that sells at 0.5% OTM has a different probability of ending the ITM.

Finally, using Delta allows you to repeat customized trades in the EDeltaPro back testing engine throughout your day trading.

3.5 Sell Options That Possess Liquidity in the Options Market

Market liquidity is crucial because you want to stay in a market where there are buyers and sellers, and the spread tight bids/inquiries, so that you can easily buy and sell your deals at the right option price. This option allows you to buy and sell on all due dates, quickly. The legitimacy of publicly traded assets is always of great concern, not only to stock traders, but also to all types of investors, companies or properties.

Liquidity mentions how "liquid" an asset is. Most "liquid" property "flows" easily and quickly by hand. The issue of liquidity in stock trading is simple, but options trading is more complicated. Determining the liquidity of options contracts is one of the most challenging problems in options trading. So, how is the liquidity choice determined? The word "liquidity" comes from the word "liquid" and is the most widely used investment terminology. Liquid flows from one place to another, and liquidity refers exactly to that state. An asset is referred to as "high liquidity" or has "high liquidity" when traded heavily and has a prepared market with ready buyers and sellers.

On the other side, when an asset is rarely sold and has fewer buyers and sellers, it is referred to as "liquid" or "low liquidity."

Generally, when you have a high liquidity asset, you can easily sell the asset for easy cash at a quickly established market price. However, when you have a tangible property, it is almost impossible to find a buyer to sell it to, and even if you do, the buyer is unlikely to buy the property at "market value" from you. Very cheap, depending on how interested you are. Although all investors understand what liquidity is and what assets or shares have good cash, measuring the liquidity of an asset is more than a science.

Ballpark figures such as an average daily trading volume of 200,000 are usually used by stock traders to mark a stock as liquid enough to sell. However, unlike securities, they actually cannot tell you how liquid contract options are, based on the amount of trade. Many options of good liquidity contracts may have little to no volume of trading within a single day. Determining liquidity opportunities can be incredibly tricky for novice traders. So, how does one establish a contract options liquidity?

An option has an expiration date at a fixed price (strike price). However, options are traded less frequently than other financial instruments, such as stocks or bonds. It makes it difficult for investors to enter the choice they want. The best way to measure option liquidity is to look at two aspects: daily volume and open interest.

The daily volume of a particular option contract is a measure of the number of times a specific agreement is contracted. The higher the daily volume, the more liquid this option is compared to the lower regular volume options. However, this option is not an accurate measure of liquidity, as each day brings a new daily volume.

Furthermore, obtaining information on past daily volumes is more challenging to get on the vast amount of available stock.

There can be illiquid options too. When market holders feel it is too dangerous to take a stake in a given option, due to lack of liquidity, options are illiquid. Alert, derivatives traders, aren't actively exchanging stocks in the options market with other options traders. Both options traders work with skilled market managers who are entrusted with the responsibility to the market, and hold value with all options contracts. These market players are still able to purchase or sell options, therefore ensuring liquidity on all contract options. It is particularly so, for very highly traded stocks like the stock company. Yeah, if the underlying stock has secure cash, the possibilities are likely to be extremely liquid. So, whose contracts are like illiquid options?

Illiquid options at a price that includes some foreign interest would be incredibly difficult to sell.

It ensures that, even though the underlying market moves in favour of the contract options, you can find it challenging to sell those options, unless you can sell at an incredibly low price.

Indeed, one typical phenomenon you might face when selling an illiquid options contract is that, when the underlying market price increases, the option's Offer price rises, but not the BID price! Yeah, you see the option getting more and more expensive to purchase, so you can't just sell it at any cheaper price, resulting in an incredibly broad bid request range. And how is it that we can say if an alternative is illiquid? What is the definitive way to measure the liquidity of contract options if both quantity and open interest are not strong measures of liquidity choices?

The more eager and nervous market owners are to buy a contract option from you, or sell it to you, the more liquid the contract options are. How do we know if market owners are willing to buy and sell a deal for particular options?

The more market players bargain to purchase and sell a contract, the more competitive a contract for options becomes. It shows up in the chain of possibilities as the bid order stretches. 'Ask price' is the price at which a market maker wants to give you a contract option, and the 'buy price' is the one at which a market maker agrees to buy the contract option from you.

Market players also bid for transactions and deals with each other. Even though it has zero volume, and next to none in terms of open demand, the smaller the bid-offer range of an options contract is, the higher the liquidity. Often, highly liquid options may have bid requests spread as narrow as $0.05, and deals for illiquid options may have bid requests spread as wide as $1.00 or more. Yes, the best predictor of liquidity options is the bid-offer distribution of contract options.

As such, the best liquidity protection you will get is an option contract with high length, open interest and narrow bid request range. As a rule of thumb, a bid-offer range of within 10 percent of the auction price is a relatively reliable indicator of liquidity. Often, stock options that are actively traded tend to be very competitive with strong bid spread speaking.

3.6 Manage Winning Trades

The management of winning trades is crucial to optimizing overall success rates. You want to realize the benefit of running late in the option life-cycle. Using Citigroup (C) as an example, say on March 20, you sold a one-month cover call during a $ 67 strike when the stock was trading at $ 65 - at the end of March/April. Initially, the stock sinks at ~ 60, providing the opportunity to close to buy, to realize weakness and profits.

However, if you wait, and by April 20, the stock has crossed $ 70, its strike price of $ 67 will cause you to abandon the capital or lose yourself in the option. Manage a win before that. You were preventing the possibility of stocks going up against you late in the option contract to realize profit and increase the success rate. You can see about 200 trades here; I manage to win between 50% -90% of Premium Capture.

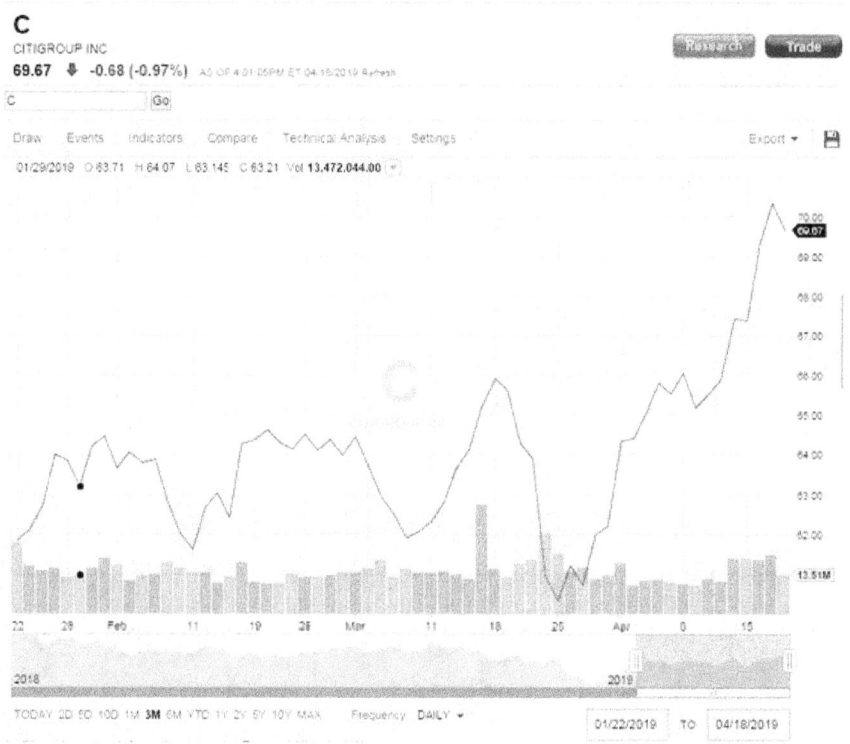

Before you enter the trade, set realistic profit goals and risk/reward ratios. What is the minimum risk/reward you accept?

Most traders do not trade unless the potential profit is at least three times the risk. If, for example, your stop-loss is $1 per share, your target profit should be, at least, $ 3 per share. Determine weekly, monthly and annual profit goals as a percentage of your portfolio in dollars, and check them regularly.

Often merchants make the mistake of spending too much on buying signals but pay no attention to when to exit. Most traders don't want to lose because they can't sell if they're down. Overcome that feeling, learn to accept the loss, or you will not make it in this business. If your stop is damaged, it means you made a mistake. Do not take it personally. Professional traders lose more trades than they win, but they still gain by managing money and limiting losses.

Before you start a trade, you should know your exit. There are at least two exits for each business. First of all, what is your stop loss if the deal goes against you? You should write it down. Second, every business should have a profit goal. Once you get there, sell some of your position, and if you wish, you can hold your area for the rest of your life.

3.7 Limit Position Sizing/Allocation

Limit the size of your allocation to keep your position at risk when the underlying protection against you is broken. This is accomplished by the diversification of tickers with various sector exposures in both stocks and ETFs, limiting each position to a 1-10% portfolio, and holding cash.

This calculation divides your capital according to the number of futures, stocks, foreign exchange, commodities, options you want to trade, number of positions or instruments you can place in your portfolio. For example, say you have a total risk of 100,000 $ capital, and you want to add five different allocations in your wallet to diversify your risk. Your instrument capital split should be the total number of risk capital/positions, in this example, area 100,000 / 5 = $ 20,000 of capital per allocation.

Typically, traders, now, incorrectly allocate the capital, dividing it by the share price. For example, if Microsoft trades 727 shares at $ 27.50: they do $ 20,000 / $ 27.50. It is a mistake because it does not take into account your stoppage or capital risk%. For example, if you do this for every five positions, you take a big risk and do not take into account the Staples or Capital Risk%.

Since 2001 it is suggested to risk 1%, or less, especially at the beginning. This percentage allows you to have 100 consecutive losing trades before blasting your account, so you have plenty of time to manoeuvre and not be emotionally attached to any single trade or situation.

So, for each instrument, the maximum risk for your business is % 1 to 1 capital allocation, in this example, 1% x $ 20,000 = $ 200 is the maximum amount you should risk at each position. In addition to the 1% rule, you need to include the final factor, the stoppage level, before calculating the correct shares.

This step is essential. It would be best if you relied on your Staples on your chart and personal trading process, not the arbitrary monetary level. So, let's say your chart technical analysis and trading strategy shows you a long signal for Microsoft, which is trading at 27.50, and if the price is less than $ 26.10, that signal is no longer valid, you decide to set $ 1.50 at his stops at $ 26.00, risk. Per-share. Now that you know that you are willing to take 50 1.50 risk per share, and you have a chance of % 200, you are ready to buy, for the allotted position, using the right number of shares to buy. The correct number of shares that can be calculate for each device has a predefined stoppage level and a pre-set capital risk %.

To calculate the maximum number of shares to buy:

Maximum $ Risk / Stop Loss Level for Trade = Maximum optimal position size.

In this example, $ 200 / $ 1.5 = 133 shares. It is the number of secured stocks higher than the 727 stocks at risk. It gives the size of the position to hedge funds and pro-traders; these position-sizing principles will keep you in the right place even if you don't have a personal trading strategy. It's safe, and it's intense - even with a poor trading strategy, the right mathematics will keep you in the game for a longer time.

Also, since you know that you will only benefit a small percentage (1% or less) of your capital, your business will be less stressful in each case, and your chart and trading process will depend on your emotions. As an outcome, you will have a better chance to achieve stability and stay in the game longer.

This comprehensive selection strategy provides the basics for a successful long-term options trading. These essentials allow you to quickly create your portfolio, because no matter how the market moves, options are not where stocks go These fundamentals provide long-term sustainable high-probability win rates that generate a steady income while reducing market momentum.

Following these option trading imperatives, I have seen the 87% option win rate in the Bull and Bear markets over the past seven months, compared to the S&P 500's margin of 6.4% over the same period.

Chapter 4: Golden Rules for Trading Successfully

Anyone who wants to become a successful stock trader should spend a few minutes online to find phrases such as "Plan your trading, trade your plan" and "minimise your risks." For new traders, these tips may seem more distracting than actionable. If you are a brand-new person in trading, you need to know how to make money quickly.

Each of the rules reported below is important, but the effects are reliable as they work together. Focusing on them will significantly increase your odds of success in the markets.

4.1 Always Use a Trading Plan

The trading plan is a set of written rules that are able to set the merchant's entry, exit, and money management criteria for each purchase. With today's automation, it is easy to test a commercial idea before real money is in danger. Back testing is a practice that allows you to apply your business idea using historical data and determine if it is viable.

Once a plan has been established, and back testing has shown excellent results, it can be used in real business.

The key here is sticking to the program. Trading outside the predetermined scheme, even if they are winners, is considered a poor strategy.

When trading as many endeavours, it's essential to start at the end and work backwards to create your plan and find out what kind of trader you are. The most successful traders will work for one idea and may even have multiple projects working together. Why is it advised to always Write Things? Because it helps you to focus on your business goals, and we need to use less judgment better. A plan can help you maintain discipline as an entrepreneur. It helps you to continually do business, manage your emotions and improve your trading strategy. It is also essential to use your plan. Most people make a plan to spend their time and never implement it again.

Make sure you do your research and create a plan that meets your needs. Find faith in what you know. The tools you choose for your strategy are the main ones, with a detailed description of the policy, from chart type to specific drawing tool. Test your plan early to make sure you are on the right track.

Once you start trading, continue to test it regularly. It allows you to measure your success to see what works and what doesn't. From there, you can add items that are weak and do not contribute to your overall goal.

Ask yourself the following questions (the answers to these will help you in the foundation of your trading plan).

If your quick answer is "to make money," you have to stop there. If the only milestone is to make as much money as we can, eventually, we will be doomed because it will never be enough. Managing your risks should be your primary goal. It creates an environment that can be profitable. How do I increase my strength to reduce my weaknesses?

An example of a weakness is always watching one's trades. Do you have your laptop on the pillow, and you watch the businesses awake at night? Making wise decisions when you are half awake is difficult. Look at things in percentage; remember that leverage is a double-edged sword. That is why risk and wealth management is critical. It is tough to determine what kind of merchant you are; the type of merchant you want to be in is very different from the sort of merchant you want based on your behaviours and characteristics.

Once you have achieved your goals, hunger, risks, strengths, and weaknesses will become apparent to you what kind of business suits you. You see three columns in the chart; they are labeled short, base, and long. Aadhaar is like a time-chart that spends most of your time, and if you're not sure, this is the time frame you are going to pursue.

The timeframe charts are short and long as you verify or reject what is happening in the base timeframe chart. It is a usual mistake for traders to jump randomly between chart timeframes.

You should start investing in education and researching yourself once you decide what kind of entrepreneur you are. Make everyday practice a priority, as each person's strategy or methodology is unique and not replicable. So, your plan will be successful depending on your individual needs. Assess your needs and the effort required. Make sure you understand why you are doing business. The initial investment is probably not monetary but will benefit you in the long term. Time and research should be a sustainable investment. Research can help you understand all aspects of the business so that you can follow current global events and keep yourself up-to-date on existing analytics tools. "Am I a fundamentalist or a tech entrepreneur?"

It is essential to create a strategy using fundamental and technical tools, but first we must learn a bit about each of these types. Some traders use fundamental analysis to help with their trading decisions—this type of study based on the news. The news can be considered anything related to economic, political, or environmental events. As a consequence, the preliminary examination is very subjective.

Other traders can use technical analysis to drive their trading decisions. This type of analysis is more conclusive and relies more on the mathematics and opportunities behind the business. Specific examples of analytics may be indicative. They may be leading or lagging. There are very few key indicators available about where the market can go. Fibonacci is the most popular but usually misused and misunderstood. Once you have decided on some types of analytics to use, it is time to develop a business strategy. It could be through fundamental analysis, technical analysis, or a combination of both. You must develop a strategy and incorporate it into your business plan.

A step-by-step systematic strategy for when and how we are going to use tools to develop the sequence of analysis. In the trading strategy, we can see:

- Types of diagnostic tools (necessary, technical or both)
- When and how diagnostic tools are used
- Last date to use the tool
- Sequence of analysis
- High potential business, detail to be seen
- Types of commands to be used

This sequence leads us to how high probability trading based on indicators and analytics. Since we have the necessary funds for our strategy, let's look at the money and risk management of trading.

Talking about money and risk management and trying to figure out how close your risk tolerance is, could be a difficult step for many people. "How much cash do I need to trade?" Be honest with what is available to you.

One mistake people make is to think that business is an investment or a grab-and-go activity and accumulate money. Trading is not a deposit and has action. Liquefaction occurs when 100% of the total margin requirements of all open positions no longer meet. There should be no more winning trades than losing moneymakers; they can only manage their losing trades so that the winners can turn them into a total profit. It is easy to win and still profitable in a short time. New traders' characteristic feature is to take advantage of it quickly, but let them loose trades. As a result, they must be at high risk for a reward ratio.

Consider in terms of probability. It helps to use the 3% rule and always have a pillow. It is an example of the 3% rule in action: 3% of a $ 10,000 account equals 300 risks per trade. Then divide the risk expense by accounting for equity, number of businesses lost, or $ 10,000 / $ 300 or 33.3 deals.

These answers will help you decide if you can achieve your goals. It allows you to give yourself space for flexibility. Merchants limit their business and planning if there is not enough space for risks. While developing your business plan and remembering other costs is essential, some may have more jolt than others, but all donations to your investment in a business plan.

We know that the time is right to start once we have set the right strategy and how much risk we have set.

Business can be everything. When do markets open up? When do they stop? What tools (e.g., currency pairs) do I trade? Some markets are open when closed, or they overlap. Some significant markets have open and closed time here. Higher volatility occurs at the start and end of the market, but also when reports or news are released. The beauty of some equipment business is the ability to trade them even if the market you live in is closed. The diagram below shows the overlap of open markets. Look at the time when more than two markets are free at once. Eastern Time From 8 am to 1 pm or 1 pm Eastern Time or 5 pm to noon; it displays the highest demands worldwide. Choosing your time for business or looking at the market is easy, as there is a possibility of opening a market elsewhere.

4.2 Protect Your Trading Capital

Saving enough cash to fund a trading account is a big part of the time and effort. If you have to do it two times, it will be more difficult.

It is crucial to note that protecting your trading capital is not synonymous with losing business. Trading is cheap for all traders. Protecting money does not cause unnecessary risk, and you can do everything to protect your commercial enterprise. Management is the key to trading and protecting your trading capital from losing trades. This lesson demonstrates the importance of implementing prudent risk management to avoid significant risks that can lead to losing your entire trading account. Risk management should start as soon as you start learning, and it should be essential in your trading career. It allows you to deal with performance slowdowns, and it protects your trading account at this point, which will enable you to trade.

The main principle of wealth management is that you should never risk too little of the money you need to trade in any one trade. Most professional traders are advised not to disclose more than 1% to 2% of the account in a single trade.

Limiting your business risk by up to 1-2% of your total account will significantly reduce the impact of losing streaks, as you will save most of your trading account.

Just a 1% risk in each trade means you can lose twenty consecutive trades and have more than 80% of your initial capital. If you take a 5% risk per trade, your original money after twenty losing trades is less than 40%.

More than 90% of people who trade in the stock market lose money and this happens because the vast majority do not use the right cash and risk management principles. Money management, position or business size. Whatever you call it, you know better!

"Money management is like sex-act: everyone does it one way or another, but most people don't want to talk about it, and others do better. Do not risk more than 2% of commercial capital in trading.

Your maximum risk is $ 600 if you have $ 30,000, but there are a lot of things to forget about, even for a brokerage. If it says $ 25 in every way, your maximum risk is now 50 550, and if your stock falls $ 550, the appropriate stop sets. Never trade with more than 20% commercial capital.

Again, if you have 30K, your trading volume is $ 6000, but if I have 5% open trades and 19% exit my trading capital market, slipping, education, data, etc.

What is the Most Common Mistake in Trading Capital?

My necessary trade using the above example is now $ 1000, up to $ 1000, so I decided to open my second trade. If the current trailing/profit stops, the right approach is to determine the value of the share. The next calculation based on $ 30,000 + $ 900, so you might be $ 1000, but your back is stuck, and if you hit low, it says $ 900. The definitive things in life are only death and taxes!" So, it should be noted that past showing is not a reliable indicator of future performance, but you can control risk.

It is the 21st century, and it is widespread to manage one's investment, and yet very disciplined professionals apply or understand the principles of wealth risk management. During the stock market boom, the risk is always a crucial factor, but because of recent volatility and market conditions, you must be serious about it!

Business money and risk management strategies, used correctly and together, can be your foundation for commercial success.

Essentially, money management tells you how many stocks to trade at any given time, and stop placement means you have to admit that you made the wrong decision, close that trade, and move on. It's a defensive concept that places you in the game to play. Don't confuse money management with stop placement. Stop placement does not solve the question.

Risk management is the difference linking success and failure when trading shares. It refers to stopping the placement and minimising any loss, and you have them, but any gains increased, and this stop is called a trailing, maintenance, or profit stop. Money management optimizes capital utilisation. Some people can view their portfolio as a whole. Fewer traders and investors also take a defensive or reactive approach to risk, in which they measure risk in an aggressive or active currency to prevent losses. The risk is more effective in investing actively. Risk Manager will assist you to do all of the above more efficiently. JBL Risk Manager is a professional but straightforward money risk management program especially developed to solve the above problem. Still, unfortunately, testing is currently only available to those who have access to metastatic format data over the Internet.

It automatically calculates a lot based on your trading volume, stop-loss price, trailing stop, break-even price, and closing price.

It allows you to convert your purchase price to the actual purchase price (slippage). It indicates when you need to look for another trade and automatically report on your performance showing your portfolio % win-loss ratio, average $ win-loss ratio, trade expectation, and more. I hope you give this program a try. After more than a decade of trying to understand the importance of money risk management for beginners and experienced people, I am delighted that this simple program is able to do just that.

There is also the option of entering a technical stop if you wish. Still, after many years of testing and research, I have found that they use technical analysis for admission and money risk for their departure. Management does precisely that. Long-term investors can use fundamental analysis to find financially healthy companies, followed by TA for entry and MR management for an exit.

4.3 Use Technology

It is safe to assume that the person who sits on the other side of the industry makes full use of all available technology.

Charting platforms give traders different ways to view and analyse markets. Supporting an idea using historical data can be rather costly.

Receiving market updates through a smartphone allows us to monitor trades anywhere. As with high-speed Internet connections, the technology we carry can highly improve business performance.

Using technology to your advantage and staying current with new products can be both fun and rewarding in business.

Experienced traders today bring a big smile to their faces when they see all available options to anyone who wants to enter the business world. Before the Internet, you could only trade by phone. If a trader calls his broker for trading, the broker must call the floor trader, who is physically present at the exchange.

Nowadays, all you need to do is a computer, trading software and a good, reliable internet connection. Every merchant needs to start somewhere, and if you are a beginner trader, Robinhood is the best place to start your business career. The app for computers, smartphones, and tablets came out in iOS in early 2015. Eight months later, it came to Android, and customers have already made more than $ 1 billion in trade.

Other than a simple interface, what makes Robinhood so impressive? The answer is simple - trade without commission. The people behind Robinhood claim their customers are saving up to $ 5 million a month in fees.

When it comes to business, you can accept that no matter how much you prepare yourself for education, others know better. There is nothing wrong with this - thousands of entrepreneurs around the world think a lot. That's where the signs come. The signal is a service provider notification of the trade that the provider thinks is beneficial. You decide whether to trade or trust all the businesses you suggested and follow them automatically.

Forex signal provider SnipeTheTrade is one of the most stellar services that allows you to copy transactions from a professional trader. The facility offers a seven-day free trial and also provides binary options signals.

You can also use Snip Trade's EA Expert Assistant to copy your foreign currency signals automatically. Currently, production has a success rate of eighty percent and above.

Some traders prefer to focus on economic events and global news to sustain their trades, while others believe that the market is predictable but possible. This forecast can be used to create algorithms that monitor market movements and respond accordingly when certain numerical conditions occur.

Flex Trader is an automated, broker-neutral trading system that acts as an implementation management tool. Merchants will be able to fully customise the algorithms available through Flex Trader, which includes only financial tools of interest.

The trading days of high-powered city dealers is approaching fast. Gamification - the process of applying gaming to real-world topics - is fast becoming a significant factor in the commercial sector, as explained in this excellent article on gamma planning.

Trade Hero is a gamified app that allows wannabe traders to throw millions of dollars in a lively atmosphere.

Trade Hero customers use the app to learn how to do business without risking their capital and see how they can become successful traders by following professional traders. They can compete with their fellow customers by using 'play money' to win trading glory. This is how we can use technology in trading to become successful.

4.4 Treat Trading Like a Business

In order to be successful, it needs to be a full or part-time business rather than a hobby or a job. If it's called a hobby, there's no real commitment to learning. If this is a job, it can be frustrating because there is no regular pay-check.

Business is a business, and there are costs, risks, taxes, uncertainties and stress. As an entrepreneur, you are necessarily a small business owner, and you need to research and strategies to increase your business potential. "Business should be considered a business."

There is some level of structure and processes on the direction the business needs to go. The same applies in trading, the moment you open your computer, the moment you leave, you run the business.

In business, many people emphasize the benefits of having a business plan. The main idea behind this is to describe what the organisation is accomplishing and how it performs against competitors. There is no difference in trading and a good plan will go a long way.

If you are serious about trading, but never take the time to plan it wisely, you will have new work on your to-do list.

You need to have a well-thought-out business plan that separates teasers from professional traders. It also changed the total income my business received did. At a time when my trading was not profitable, I severely altered and made a trading plan.

Please see my guide to the Final Trading Plan if you want more information on writing a good trading plan. Keep in mind that the trading plan does not need to be hyper-long (or use boring and useless words).

However, this plan will be your primary business document. It includes all the facts you start to the moment you finish your workday.

If you already have a commercial plan, congratulations, you have taken the first step to do business like a pro!

Some businesses are recognised for their careful planning phase. In the process, people see how things will work out in the future. It looks good until the end of the plan.

In trading, you must take some time to plan your trading strategy. It means researching, defining your policy, and making it one step further. You may be surprised at how difficult it is to implement your approach to the advantage.

However, one thing must be mentioned. You have to be very careful. There is not enough planning and prepare yourself to fail. Plan too much, and you will never reach your goal. Do it in trading and plan for a limited period of your choice, as mentioned earlier. Think about those annual assessments at work that review employee achievements and company success. It's a business that needs to find ways to improve for the next year. By deleting your journal review, you can adjust your strategy to improve it. I recommend that traders review their journal at least every month, every week to get a glimpse of what has happened in the last few weeks.

Although you can trade your business in many other ways, you can do things to improve your business planning, scheduling meetings, carefully planning, and reviewing your trades.

By applying these elements to your business, you are almost guaranteed to see improvement in a short period of time.

Remember that nothing here should be as fancy as merchandise. Often, I have noticed that companies are more concerned with the amount of paperwork than the quality and meaning of the content. Try to do the opposite and keep it simple!

Write down your ideas about yourself and business values. Determine your talents, your wealth, and your skills. Determine the obstacles you face and how you can solve them.

Next, assess the number of financial freedoms and develop a plan to reduce the quantity to zero. When you have done this, it is possible to do more research, so you will devote your life to do something that you love. See my book Secure Strategies for Financial Freedom to know more about the financial freedom number. Based on the mastery of who you are, decide your trading targets. What are your goals as a trader?

Primary applications for any company. There are a lot of tools needed to run a trading business other than trading systems.

You have to gaze at the different structures to assess the following:

How do you sell and communicate with customers? How do you keep track of the cash flow? How do you keep an eye on the back office? The deals? Were you mistaken? What's your intention to conduct continuing work into trading systems?

Preparing the Strategy:

- Study on market-related trading tactics.

- Find out objectively what will operate in that sort of business.

- List possible success targets.

- List your beliefs about the business.

- Determine the trading time frame that best suits you for that sort of market.

Perform this step for each of the various forms of business — upwards, downwards, and sideways, in calm and unpredictable conditions. You will need to build at least three entry-level programs, decide your initial vulnerability, and evaluate your exits from benefit taking. How are you going to do this? What suggestions are you having at the moment?

4.5 Study the Markets

Think about it in terms of higher education. Traders must keep focused on learning more every day. It's important to remember that understanding the markets, and all their intricacies, is a lifelong process that keeps going on.

Hard research enables traders to understand the facts, just like what the various economic reports mean. Focus and observation give traders the ability to sharpen their intuition and understand the nuances.

Global affairs, world stories, global trends — even the weather — have a business effect. The local business is competitive. The earlier merchants grasp the economies of the past and present, the more positioned they are to face the future. World markets are attracting speculative capital like moths to a flame, with the majority of the money thrown at securities without understanding why prices are moving upwards or downwards.

Instead, they are following hot ideas, taking conditional calls and sitting at gurus' feet, letting them purchase and sell choices that make no sense. A safer course is to learn how to skillfully and authoritatively navigate the markets.

Start with a self-examination, which takes a close look at your money relationship.

Do you see life as a challenge, involving a hard effort to earn every dollar? Would you agree that personal magnetism can draw your business's wealth in the same way it brings to other pleasures of life? More ominously, do you routinely lose money through different operations, and hope that the financial markets will treat you nicer?

Papers on the economy. Books on the stock market. Tutorials on the website. There's a wealth of knowledge out there, the majority of it is inexpensive to use. And don't pay attention too narrowly on one single trading aspect of the game. Instead, research whatever is considered market-wise, including theories and topics that you don't think, is especially important. Trading begins a trip that always ends up at the starting line to a not expected destination. Your sincere and detailed business knowledge can come in handy from time to time again, while you feel you know just where you are going right now.

Research the fundamentals of economic forecasting, then study demand maps in all periods, thousands of them. You may think that fundamental research provides a safer road to benefit as it measures curves of growth and income sources. Still, traders live and die through pricing activity that sharply diverges from underlying fundamentals. Do not avoid reading spreadsheets from business, as they bring a trade advantage to others who neglect them.

They will not allow you to survive your first year as a trader, though. Your familiarity with charts and technical modelling is now taking you into the exciting world of price predicting. In general, shares may either go higher or lower, facilitating alongside buy or a short sale. Prices can do many other things, as well as chopping sideways at a time for weeks or vigorously whipping in both directions, shaking buyers and sellers out.

Now is the time to get your feet wet without giving up your trading value. Paper trading, or computer trading, provides an ideal alternative, allowing the neophyte to observe market activity in real-time, make purchasing and selling decisions that form the outline of an academic record of results. It typically includes the use of a simulator on the stock market and has the look and sound of the results of a real stock exchange.

Create lots of trades, using various holding times and techniques, and then evaluate the outcomes for apparent flaws.

So, when are you proceeding to make the switch and start doing real money with trading? There is no correct solution because simulated trading holds a mistake that is sure to emerge when you start trading for real, even though the results of your paper look good. Traders need a peaceful coexistence with the twin emotions of greed and fear.

Trading in the paper doesn't engage these emotions, which can only experience through actual profit and loss. This psychological dimension, in return, drives out of the game more first-year players than poor decision-making. Your baby is moving forward as a new trader needing to recognise this challenge and address the remaining money and self-worth issues.

Though experience is a beautiful teacher, don't neglect additional schooling following your career in the industry. Both online or in person, courses can be useful. They can see at levels ranging from novices (with guidance on how to interpret, for example, the aforementioned analytical charts) to pro.

More specialised seminars can provide valuable insight into the overall market and specific investment strategies, often conducted by a professional trader. The majority of the focus is on a particular type of asset, one specific market aspect, or a trading technique. Some may be scientific, and others may be more like seminars where you deliberately take positions, test entrance and exit strategies, and other (often with a simulator) drills.

It can be both educational and useful to pay for research and analysis.

Any investors may find it more valuable to watch or study market practitioners than to try to apply the newly learned lessons themselves. A slew of paid subscription sites is available over the web.

You need to discuss role and risk management once you are up and running with real money. Each position carries a holding period and technical parameters that favour targets for profit and loss, requiring your timely exit once reached. Now imagine the mental and practical strains of holding three to five positions at a time, with some heading in your direction, while others are loading in reverse.

Fortunately, there is plenty of room to study all facets of market administration, as long as you don't overload yourself with so much knowledge. If you haven't already done so, now is the time to create a regular newspaper that records all your transactions, including the explanations for risk-taking, as well as keeping times and final profit or loss figures. These events and insights diary lay the groundwork for a trading edge that will end your beginner status and encourage you to take money out of the market reliably. Begin your trading path with a comprehensive stock market education, read charts and observe price movements, and create plans based on your comments. Test these strategies with paper trading, analysing results, and making adjustments continuously.

Then complete the first leg of your trip with a monetary risk that will force you to address issues of trade management and market psychology.

4.6 Always Use a Stop Loss

A stop loss is a set amount of risk a trader is willing to embrace with each trade. The stop loss can be a dollar quantity or percentage, but anyway, it limits the trader's exposure during a deal.

Using a stop loss will take some of the risks out of trading because we know that we will lose X number on any given transaction.

It's the best luck not to have a stop loss even though it leads to a winning deal. Exiting with a stop loss, and therefore making a losing deal, because it comes under the guidelines of the trading program, is indeed a successful deal.

The goal is to leave with an income from both trades, but this is not possible. Using a loss defensive stop helps to make sure injuries and risks are reduced.

Firstly, the beauty of the stop-loss order is that it doesn't cost anything to implement.

Your regular commission will only charge once the price of the stop-loss reached, and the stock has to sell. You might think of it as a policy for free insurance.

Most importantly, a stop-loss allows to free decision-making from any emotional influences. People continue to fall in love with stocks, assuming it will come back if they give a share of another shot. It causes procrastination and uncertainty, which can only allow losses to accumulate by offering the stock yet another chance.

Whatever type of investor you are, you should be aware of why you buy a warehouse. The criteria for a value investor will differ from the one of a growth investor, which will still be different from an active trader. Any strategy can work, but only if you adhere to that strategy. It also means that the stop-loss orders are next to zero unless you are a committed buy-and-hold trader.

The aim here is to have faith in your plans and to bring the approach forward. Stop-loss orders can benefit you to stay on track without emotionally clouding your judgment.

Finally, it is necessary to remember that stop-loss orders do not ensure that you will be making money on the stock market; you do have to make sound investing decisions. If you don't, you're going to lose much money as if at a slower rate without a stop-loss.

Stop-loss instructions traditionally conceived of as a way of reducing losses, hence their nickname. However, another application of this method is to lock in earnings, in which case it is often referred to as a "trailing hold." Here, the stop-loss order is placed at a percentage point below the actual selling price, not the amount you bought.

The stop-loss price adjusts with fluctuating stock prices. Remember, if capital goes up, what you have is an unrealised obtain, which means that you do not have the amount in hand until you sell. Using a trailing stop permit you to let profits run while guaranteeing at least some realised capital gain at the same time.

Continuing with our example from above, say you set a trailing stop order 10 percent below the current cost and the stock skyrockets at $30 a month. You will then lock in the trailing-stop order at $27 a share ($30-(10 percent x $30) = $27). Because that is the worst price you'd get, even if the stock takes an unexpected dip, you're not going to be in the red. Of course, keep in mind that the stop-loss order is still a market order — it simply stays dormant and is only activated when the price of the trigger is reached — so the price at which your sale trades may be slightly different from the price of the trigger given.

The benefit of a stop-loss order is that you don't have to monitor how each day a stock performs. This convenience is particularly useful when you're on holiday or in a situation that stops you from watching your shares for a relatively long period.

The only drawback is that a short-term fluctuation in stock price could trigger the stop price. The trick is to pick a percentage stop-loss that helps a stock to fluctuate from day to day while minimising as much chance of downside as possible. It is not the safest technique to place a 5 percent stop loss on a stock with a history of fluctuating 10 percent or more in one week. More likely, you'll only lose money on the commission created by implementing your stop-loss order.

The level at which stops can put is not subject to hard-and-fast rules. That depends solely on the particular investment style: an aggressive trader may use 5 percent, while a long-term investor can use 15 percent or more.

Another thing to remember is that your stop order is a market order after you hit your stop price and the price you sell, which varies a lot from the stop price. This fact is particularly actual in a fast-moving market where stock prices can swiftly change. Another limitation with the stop-loss order is that many brokers will not allow you to place a stop order on individual securities, such as stocks on the OTC Bulletin Board or penny stocks.

Stop-limit orders bear additional possible threats. These orders can guarantee a cost limit, but it might not be possible to carry out the trade. It can harm investors when the stop order triggers the fast market, but the limit order not filled before the market price blasts through the limit price. If lousy news arises about a company and the limit price is only $1 or $2 below the stop-loss price, the investor must hold onto the stock for an indefinite period before the share price rises again. Both types of orders can be entered either as day orders or as good-until-canceled orders (GTC).

A stop-loss order is a secure method, but it is not used successfully by many investors. Almost all investment styles can benefit from this trade, whether to prevent excessive losses or to lock in profits. For example, think of a stop-loss as an insurance policy: You are sure you'll never have to need it, so it's good to think you've got the cover.

4.7 Develop a Trading Methodology

The initiative is worth taking the time to establish a sound trading technique. It might be enticing to think that the scams that are widespread on the internet are "so simple it is like printing money." But facts should be the inspiration behind developing a trading plan, not emotions or hope.

Traders who are not in a rush to know usually have an easier time sifting through all the online material. Consider this: if you were to begin a new career, you would certainly need to study for almost a year or two at a college or university before you were even qualified to apply for a new field position. Learning how to trade requires at least the same amount of time and research and study driven by facts.

There are plenty of outstanding trading techniques, and buying some books will save your time to find one that fits, but trading is something that can also be a profession of like "do it yourself." Many trading buyers might spend hundreds of dollars or even thousands for searching for a perfect trading strategy, but it can be exciting, simple, and shockingly quick to create your own.

You will need access to plans or charts to make a strategy that reflects the time frame to be an exchange, a curious mind, and a paper to list your ideas. You then ratify these ideas into a strategy, and on other charts, "visually back test" them. Once you have ended that, you will start creating your own strategies in any trading market.

It would assist if you narrowed down the options in chart before a strategy can create. Are you a day trader, an investor, or a swing trader? Be sure to pick a time frame that fits your needs.

Then, you're going to want to pay attention to which market you're going to trade: forex, stocks, options, or commodities? If you have picked any time period and price, determine which form of trading you would like to do. For example, if you select to look for goods for day-trading purposes on a 1-minute timeframe and want to mainly concentrate on stocks that move within a small range or you can deploy a goods screener for shares currently traded within a specific range and meet other requirements like pricing criteria and min volume.

Stocks move over time frame, so when needed, run new screens to search stocks that match according to your trading criteria once the former stocks are no longer trading in a matches trading strategy.

Creating a workable strategy makes it much harder to adhere to your trading plan because it is the tactic. Suppose a day trader, for example, decides to stocks over a five-minute time frame.

The trader will follow the ups and downs to see if anything has precipitated those movements. All indicators are evaluated, such as time frame of a single day, chart patterns, mini-cycles, candlestick patterns, volume. When a suitable approach is discovered, it helps to see if the same thing happens on the map on other moves. Could this method have made a profit over the last day, week, or month?

If you're trading on a 5-minute time frame, keep looking at only five minutes, but look in time that have same criteria to see if they'd also work there.

Once you've established a series of guidelines that will encourage you to enter the market, make a profit, look at the same situations and see what the risk will be.

To gain income without being interrupted, decide what the stops would need to be on future transactions. Analyse cost movement after entry, and see where a stop should be placed on your charts — looking for profitable exit points when you analyse the moves. What was the perfect escape stage, and which measure or tool should be used to catch more of this activity?

You can search for tactics that work over short periods. Short-term anomalies often occur, which enable you to extract consistent profits. Such techniques cannot last more than several days but are sure to be seen again in the future.

Keep note of all the tactics you use in a report and use them in a marketing plan. If situations for a particular approach turn undesirable, you should prevent it. You can capitalise on that in the market when conditions favour a strategy.

The use of empirical statistics and seeking a workable approach won't guarantee profitability in none of the markets.

Many traders are not supporting their plans by using the historical data strategy. They prefer to do random exchanges, instead. That is an absence of due diligence.

Understanding the success rate of policy is crucial because if a plan never succeeded, it's not likely it will unexpectedly start working today. That's why visual back testing-looking over maps and adding new approaches to the data you have in the chosen time frame is essential.

Many approaches don't last forever. Many are sliding in and out of productivity, and that is why we should make good use of those who do work. If it has been working for the past several months, even for the past few decades, it will for sure work tomorrow. But if you never looked at the past and tested the technique, you may not even know it was there, or you may lose the confidence to use it and make money in the market's tomorrow. Moreover, realising that anything has worked in the past would also give the trade a psychological boost.

Remember that you don't have to look for approaches that work 100 percent of the time. You'll probably find no workable strategies if you do. Look for tactics netting a return at the day end, week or year, depending on the time period.

Strategies may fall in and out of fashion over several time frames; improvements sometimes needed to suit the new environment and our circumstances.

Create your plan or use someone else's to test it on a time frame that fits your preference. You will give yourself some fantastic starting points by looking back to make more money and prevent mistakes as you get more experience. Track all the techniques you use to be able to employ those tactics again when situations support them.

4.8 Risk only what You can Afford

Make sure all the money in that trading account is truly expendable before you start using real cash. If not, then the trader will try to save until it is.

Money in a trading account will not earmark for college tuition or mortgage payment for the baby. Traders will never encourage themselves to believe that they borrow capital from these other significant obligations. Losing capital is pretty upsetting because it is money that would never have invested in the first place.

The word "afford" is the most critical part of the sentence. It has nothing to do with how much money you spend, but about "impact." What impact would you have if your investment were to lose value?

Any investment you make is at risk of not yielding the returns you want it to produce. The higher the profits you expect, the higher the likelihood that you generally take in getting those returns. Taking more risk allows you to get higher returns while taking less risk reduces the chance to get higher returns.

The effect of a gamble is even more critical — in other words, what you would be willing to lose with a payoff opportunity, and how long will you handle keeping the loss. To find out the solution to this question, you have to ask yourself what will happen if the value of your investment dropped today.

When the amount of all the funds in your checking account drops, it will have a significant effect on you. Even if you have enough capital saved in a portfolio to keep it there for ten years (also known as a 10-year time horizon), the effect of a normal fluctuation will be marginal. You still don't even care!

By finding ways to reduce a risk's impact, you may be able to accept a higher chance of loss in the longer term, for a higher return. An extended period is one way to take more risks while raising the risk's future effects. It is particularly true when you pair the long-term outlook with diversification (more on that in a second).

Let's presume you have some money you want to invest, so you don't mind waiting for your ten-year returns.

If it's a reasonably risky property, over those ten years, it will gain and lose interest quite a bit — but anything that happens in the second, third, fourth, or ninth year won't impact you.

Of course, there is always the investing risk that doesn't deliver you the returns you expect over the ten-year term. But you don't have to overthink the ups and downs along the way, by planning for longer times.

In the short and medium-term, you can afford to let the investment lose value, as long as it increases value in the long run. You also assume that the underlying investment has the potential to achieve that growth. Keeping an investment, for example, in an organisation that needs to start operating video stores as its primary industry and creativity might not be ideal — but Netflix performed fine! Diversification is another means of making the value you can afford to increase. Let's say you need to pay $100. If you bring the whole $100 into one investment that has a high probability of losing any of its value, the effect of the high risk is pretty high — in the very worst scenario, you could lose all of your $100.

If you split the $100 into two pieces and put one into a risky investment and one into a less risky investment, you'd slash the future effect by half.

You 're more likely to lose $50 than the whole $100 (although there's always a chance you're missing the entire thing).

You can then divide this up as many times as you want — you can even invest in a fund to divide it into 500 or more chunks!

The argument is, diversification helps reduce the possible effect of losing interest from just one investment option. The likelihood of it losing value does not change, but it does have an impact on you.

So, if you look at it this way, the sentence we began with is valid. One way to the effect of the chances you take is to save capital that you don't care about wasting, but it's not the only way.

By planning over a more extended period and ensuring you have balanced the exposure by diversification, you can accomplish the same goal, spend more, and gain access to better returns.

4.9 Know when to Stop Trading

There are two explanations for when to stop trading: an inefficient business strategy and an ineffective investor.

The unsuccessful trading strategy reveals much more significant losses than previous research has expected. That is what happens. Markets could have changed, or volatility could have lessened.

The trading strategy simply doesn't work as planned, for some reason. Live businesslike and unemotional. It's time to re-evaluate the trading plan and make a couple of changes or start with a new business plan. A failing trading plan is a problem that needs to be addressed. It's not the end of the world. An inefficient trader is one that has a business strategy but cannot execute it. Anyone may encounter this issue through social tension, bad behaviour, and lack of physical activity. A dealer who's not in optimal market condition should consider taking a rest. The trader will return to business after any problems and obstacles have resolved.

Generally, as people understand how to exchange, they concentrate on when to transfer; however, learning when to trade is essential (if not more important).

It is just as important to know when to avoid trading. It is complicated – if you leave too early, you might miss out on any winners, but if you don't stop in time, you might lose the winners. So, it sounds good to know when to stop, but how do we know when that is?

It can be harder to identify the equilibrium between both in the hope of a good outcome and that the losses will suit the strategy. Unfortunately, as it is mostly subjective, there is no hard and fast rule on that.

You have to remind yourself how much money you have. What is your chance, and how much you might lose? How much focus and intensity of the emotion are you getting? With practice, you'll get a great sense of when and where to stop. The most important thing is that, with one deal, you don't deplete your resources entirely – control the risk, and you can continue to sell another day.

There are two prospects for that. Many traders tend to try for more significant profits on a single trade or a couple of businesses and will spend more time on those trades to make sure they become big winners. Many traders choose a more significant number of smaller deals, so the gains add up over time.

Whatever technique you want, overtrading is not the problem. Place your goals and have a strategy—check your market exposure. Stop trading after you have reached your targets. Tomorrow is a new day, and you will start over again, but overtrading now usually leads to losses.

We've thought about whether to stop dealing on a given day up to now. It's essential to learn, however, whether you can cease trading entirely – that is, leave. It's not easy to choose the right time to stop because people always stop when things get rough, so that can be just when success rolls in. There are times, however, that it is necessary to quit.

You can't see any potential functional trading result. You felt continually confused and pessimistic about your company. Trading chooses your wellbeing or the family.

Your investing has a detrimental effect on your financial condition, meaning either your family is struggling or your mental health is compromised.

Both are red flags. At the very least, take a gap from trading to rest, relax, and recharge. Save some trading money, revaluate your goals, and focus on your failures and achievements.

Consider that when relying upon your intuition and objectivity to devise a new trading approach. Instead, you might be able to try again. Sure, the stocks do not go anywhere because you take a rest, and you don't need to leave forever.

4.10 Keep Trading in Perspective

When trading, stay focused on the big picture. We should not be surprised by a losing trade; it is part of it. A winning deal is only one step on the road to a profitable business. The accumulated earnings are what makes a difference.

When a trader acknowledges wins and losses as part of the market, feelings would have less impact on the trading's success.

That's not to say we can't be enthusiastic about an especially fruitful deal, but we need to note that a losing agreement is never far away.

Setting realistic targets is a crucial part of keeping trading in perspective. In a reasonable amount of time, your business should be earning a reasonable return. If you're planning to be a multi-millionaire by Tuesday, you're setting up for disaster.

The learning process of successful trading is undoubtedly not a short one.

It takes time, similar to virtually all other endeavours based on skills. Whether it is sporting, playing a musical instrument, or martial arts.

Even though we want to become black belt traders or virtuoso price action readers in a jiffy, the timetable from here to success would not be as quick as you would like in 99 percent of cases.

It's common for us to lose perspective and get off the rails because of the extended travel time from A to B.

Putting things inside out

Look at the graph below. What you see is an immediate snapshot of an equity curve from one of the approaches in my market action path.

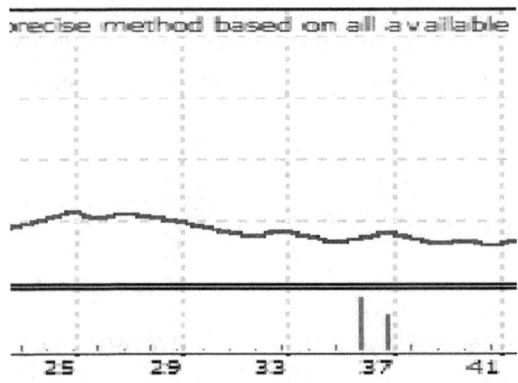

It looks incredibly unimpressive at first glance that he loses money. And in this assumption, you'd be right for this period.

Look now at the second image below, which is the complete equity curve over several years.

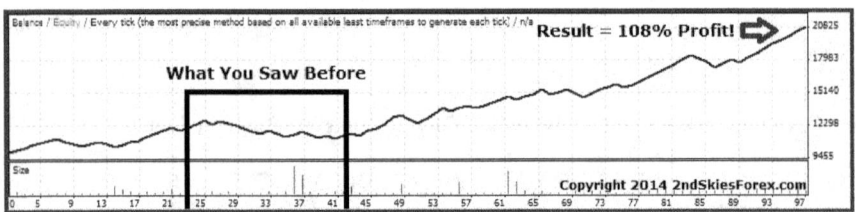

What you are doing now is something entirely new.

Looking at it as a whole, you see a price action strategy that returned 108 percent! There is just ONE PAIR across, in ONE TIME FRAME.

Here are some highlights of the results:

Gain +108.9 percent

Gain Ratio of 2.3

Payoff expected on 112.28

Total 14.27 percent drawdown

68.04 percent Profitable Trades

Most magnificent 36% Higher than the most significant loss

Max Consecutive Profit Nearly 200% Larger than Max Consecutive Loss

It is undeniably a technique that continuously makes money, retains wealth, and balances cost to reward ratio.

Below is the performance comparison table, which shows you the same results.

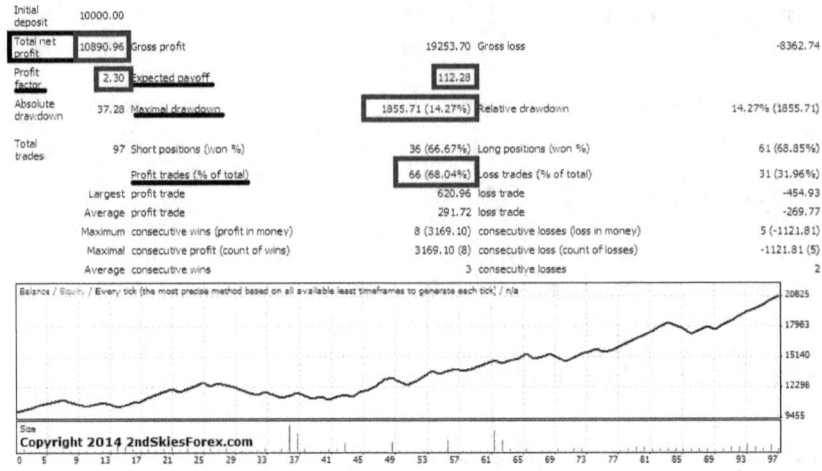

For those that don't transact profitably, most likely while you're in a drawdown, you don't allow ample room for the plan to work itself out. You see, the equity curve dropping, and you think that something has to change.

The strategy could not be wrong. Perhaps this particular strategy is not going to do well in that specific market, but over time this price action strategy is making profits.

Now imagine if at the end of the first graph you were changing strategies. You'd lost out on more than 85 percent of the overall income the plan made. You'd lose reliably profitable trade for many years. That alone would have put your 5 percent of all traders in the top spot. Build a healthy outlook.

Developing traders are generally more hypersensitive to every single trade, every win, and loss. But look at it from another angle: imagine being a new archer with the same approach – that you gage your trust based on every arrow. That map would be all over the place, driving a person batty about how they're doing, because in the beginning, of course, one will be an inconsistent shooter.

Look then at a great player in basketball, and tell me if their confidence wanes from missing one free throw. They don't make that mistake. By focusing on the process, they keep the right outlook and attitude, not a consequence. They maintain the correct viewpoint.

Constantly changing strategies every week or so will take you around in circles (like a dog chasing his tail).

Quarterbacks do not change the motions of throwing each month, nor do musicians change instruments every time things go wrong. Why would you believe there's any other route to suitable trading?

To avoid a monthly change in your trading plan and strategy, keep on to the one you've had for at least 90 days until you've perfected it. Stick to learning/trading inside and outside.

By doing so, you are building (at least) a skill set towards successful trading. And if the plan isn't working out, you're cultivating one of the most essential trading skills-disciplines.

And confidence comes with discipline, which is something lacking by most unsuccessful traders. Note, drawing down the first map was the prelude to return to 108 percent doubling the account in a couple of years.

Ask yourself if you did this after a small losing period, strategies changed. Ask yourself if you have focused more on the outcome than on the operation. Then see if that can be adjusted to maintain the correct viewpoint as you trade.

Understanding the importance of each trading rule and how they work together can help a trader set up a viable trading business. Trading is hard work, and in a very competitive environment, traders who have the ability and endurance to obey these rules will maximise their chances of success.

Chapter 5: Tips to Become a Successful Trader

Productive traders are diligent, and in general, a deficient number of traders make profits and tend to sell less than 10 percent). While trading or forex trading, there is a learning curve, so if you don't have enough start-up capital or do your homework, you start at a significant downside.

Nevertheless, as practicing to run a marathon, if you take the right measures and get the correct preparation, you are likely to succeed.

Success takes patience, preparation, and real commitment, but with the individual objects in mind. Mastering the penny stock market is beyond your grasp with the correct instruction, training, and motivation, if you practice more and more.

The path to becoming a good dealer, from any walk of life, is fully available. Still, I would reiterate that the point is that you have to be able to bring your schooling and training into the time and effort.

5.1 Start with Sufficient Capital

You must have enough money, do not spend while you're in debt. If you're looking to make small trades or micro lots, you can quickly start selling when you've got $1,000. Little capital brings emotional dealing, and this is a tragic formula. Start-up capital is a financial commitment to creating a new business or company.

The word is often used interchangeably with seed money. Still, seed money is always a more manageable amount used to build a business strategy or a project that can pass muster with venture capital investors. Understand your customer base, your product ins, and outs and what customers like and dislike. If you haven't already (and we hope you have), create a strategic plan detailing the actions you're going to take and the targets you're looking to accomplish. You are in a weak bargaining position without developing a consistent business model. You should practice your pitch too. Predict future investor questions and be prepared to answer them frankly and with facts. Indeed, being able to view your financial reports would please prospective customers and convince them that you are professional. You'll be able to show both future sales and development statistics.

Capital raising is like steps to ascend, and any action you take will increase your value. The product's concept to customers uses an organisation to join a team; each step leads to the next.

As you climb each level, your milestones determine how to approach the next phase of increasing your valuation by one step closer.

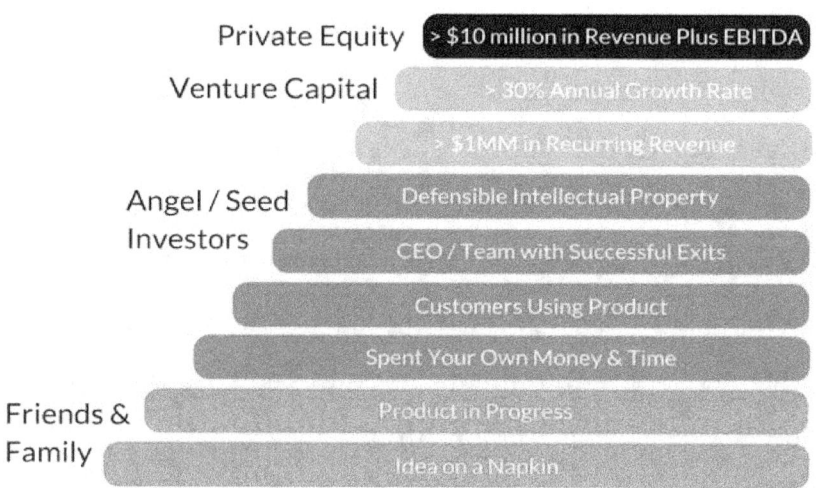

Bear in mind: you lose a tiny share of your business's equity every time you collect. You also want to consider how much capital you will need to attain each goal at each step. Know your boundaries in every step, and decide when to move on. Go at the right stage of your business, after the right investors. You'll keep going and seed investors with friends and family, and then eventually move to VC.

It's not linear to collect funds, even though it seems so. It's more of a step-function; you hit every tier of the way with milestones.

By now, you know you can never sign anything until you have thoroughly read it. When you're at a point where you're willing to consider deals, you'll be able to grasp the deal. Go over the terms and conditions and imagine reading at the paperwork (i.e., a judge, advisory council, or counsellor who was in your shoes before) for the second pair of eyes. Look at the documentation listed on the Y Combinator site to make sure you have a clear understanding of how you could influence by a price, a discount, or expectations down the line and understand what both parties get out of the deal, too. What is your lender/investor obligations, and what are their requirements for you? Knowing it would help clear the way for a real relationship.

Will you pay interest in your company, offer equity, or both? There's always something to expect in return for the investment. Know what's best for you and more realistic to commit. Doing this will ensure you are manageable and ultimately successful in your obligations. Another incentive to pay heed to the expense of the capital investment? Know your ultimate comeback.

Be sure the valuations are where you need them to be. If your value has a limit, it can be unfair for the firm if your assessment goes beyond the mark.

If you've seen success in your market, it might be time to venture capitalist on board.

Think regarding raising VC as equivalent to recruiting a supervisor. If you go down the VC path, you'll probably find a partner who wants to exert some influence over your business. As you explore this choice, consider who you'd like to partner with and search at issues like how you have a shared dream and whether this partner blends into the company culture. Have a plan, and be prepared, whatever your decision is.

While raising money may seem daunting, it is what makes day-to-day operations run smoother and more efficiently. If you have earned enough money, you're well on the way to building a thriving company that's poised to take on the industry. Nothing will hinder you.

The companies that arise when entrepreneurs have minimal resources, usually have specific characteristics and follow the alternative mentality for new venture development.

They often fall into one or more particular categories: operation, activities, results, brokerage, or education.

Service businesses rely on the skill and resources of the individual starting the company. Such a person can put their ability at the disposal of others with relatively little upfront investment. It would be best if you solely had the tools of your trade to start a service company.

A consultant might require a computer, some tools from a handyman, and a sewing machine from a dressmaker. You will use those tools on hand to start marketing your business using your contacts. Event-based companies are much more nuanced but can still launch with minimal resources (see Entrepreneur's March edition for a section on event-based companies). Businesses that are focused on activities include projects that bring on athletic competitions, festivals, and concerts. The benefit of these ventures is that with successful promotion, tickets will sell until you absorb the high costs, reducing the amount of money required to keep the company afloat.

Performance-based companies rely on entrepreneurs' abilities to succeed and bring other people together who can boost the results.

Education is another field that people with few to no money pursue opportunities. Anyone with the skills and insights would like to learn and a passion for helping others develop could move into education.

The key is, to begin with, what you currently have – the resources you can access, the ability you can leverage, and the connections at your disposal – to help you figure out a low-cost path to a new business that is sustainable and profitable.

5.2 Trading Isn't Easy Money

Gain a part-time job if you're looking for easy money. Do not start selling with the intent to get out of debt or to make money instantly. Emotions will get you to trade with too much risk involved.

Looking at a price chart — whether it's for a stock, a foreign currency pair, or a futures contract — it seems like making money should be relatively easy. When day traders get started, they often focus their attention on the significant movements and think, "If I got in there, I could have made a fortune."

Adopting such mindset will cause many people to assume that day-trading is relatively easy and a quick way to riches.

Day trading will offer considerable income if you know how to do it. For most people, however, the required amount of time spent learning and practicing prevents them from gaining enough experience to make their trades consistently profitable.

Turning a profit by day trading is a struggle because while any day trader claims that they can make profits, most people who seek to sell they end up with a net loss. By concern the risks that can lead to failures, and by getting past the assumption that day trading is secure, you can improve your odds of profitable trading.

The fact that one factor trader could lose money is the lack of a sound trading strategy. The quick retrospective glance at a map is not a successful way to build a productive approach. It can be used in many market shapes if you develop a robust strategy and can even notify you when to stay out of the market because the forms are not favourable.

A successful plan will help train you to take steps before, and not until, a lucrative opportunity occurs. Your strategy 's aim should be to uncover patterns and trends, pointing to trade opportunities that could yield positive returns.

Otherwise, your results could be determined mainly by chance without doing that research.

Many novice traders fail to understand that it takes a long time to learn to trade on a day. Putting in a couple of hours of work without investing time to day trading does not make anyone a good trader.

You may continue to conduct day-trading while holding another career because you have funds put aside for several months or longer to finance your expenses. It is highly uncommon for day traders to generate earnings right when they start. The majority of day traders don't see their struggle result in insufficient profits for many months to pay themselves any type of income.

Numerous issues and situations are helping to make it difficult for the market to gage and navigate. Taking hours to learn and understand what triggers trade activity shifts can better prepare you for those changes.

Learn to manage your financial burden if you make a false judgment about a trade path by putting an end to your trade loss.

Think of it as setting a floor to help minimise the amount of money that you may risk when seeking opportunities to trade.

Understand that when you trade, especially with market orders, you can't always get the exact price you want. The substantial trading activity could drive a price away from your precise target before you can react. You can choose to skip what may still be a good trade or accept the market price that is less than ideal. Both options will reduce your theoretical commercial profit. And if you use limit orders, you can get loaded out on winning trades for just a portion of your order the market races away before finishing the whole order. But end up with complete positions on your losers the price swings against you, and you still get the entire order.

Understand that the market is entirely composed of others trying to make money or to fend off losses (hedgers). People who are very good at trading look to profit from the orders placed by inexperienced traders.

Veteran traders are searching for rates that they think allow them to exploit any value in the commodity that others have ignored and provided them with a good entry point or exit point.

Day traders' individual preferences and goals may have a significant impact on the results of their actions. A bit of success will lead to selfish acts that are distracted from an existing business strategy. It may include moving too fast, hanging on to a lucrative income too long, or not cutting profits in a losing transaction as early as possible.

Fear will also lead day traders to hold off too much when a chance is in the making. They may also be selling in panic in response to breaking news without considering all the other factors. Creating a good trading plan has the tremendous benefit of keeping you focused on the results without being influenced by emotions.

Trading has no guarantees other than we're going to suffer the good, bad, and the ugly as we navigate the shark-infested waters. Traders can consider future rewards a risk.

Our trading journey starts with an accumulation of money as we learn and put the production of our trading strategies and style into at least 10,000 hours of practice.

It's essential to regulate our nerves and emotions if we are going to play this game and win. If we are unprepared for the fact that we will lose money, then we are done before we start.

The game's name is Results. Keep the size of trade appropriate to the size of our account. Losers scratch, take on small losses, win with trailers, it sounds easy but it's not.

Trading is a company that is going to test our spirit. Only the brightest and best get to play this game for any lengthy time. To interact for an impartial and conscious mind, with both the right rational brain and the left emotional hand, we must keep realising that trading is not easy money.

5.3 Build Your Own Success Strategy

You can buy trading systems, but they are not going to be 100 percent accurate at all times. You may find success if you rely on someone's system or you may be stuck in a losing order. To figure out what works, you should build your own method and strategy.

A lot of advertisers are selling fast money-making solutions, and those solutions are not performing well. As a forex trader, the best way to find success is to learn from your mistakes and successes, building a system along the path you can follow.

Before starting, an investor should know what they want when formulating an investment strategy at the end of it. If an investor has a target set, the investor will give more discipline to stick to it. For example, an investor might also want to set a short-term goal of buying some amount of in-demand stock shares, such as Amazon (NYSE: AMZN). An investor may also set a long-term objective of increasing its portfolio by 15 percent over one year. A trading strategy will help target an investor and achieve that goal sooner. Once they have a plan, an investor can test it out. Back testing a trading strategy could be useful in testing the framework for a test strategy.

In addition to setting a realistic trading goal, an investor will have to decide how much time they can devote to an investment plan. If an investor has little time to spend in the day, the best alternative could be the fast operation of day trading. If investors want to follow a long-term approach, they will position trades in swing trading over a more extended period. Investors should also decide on a fixed period per day to invest and keep track of their investing goals.

When a trader knows how much time they need to spend on investing, they will pick which market they want to engage.

Traders on the New York Stock Exchange or NASDAQ may also want to concentrate on US stocks. Traders seeking to consider other options should swap foreign currency (forex) or futures.

When placing a trade, an investor must determine how much money they are willing to risk. Ideally, an investor shouldn't risk more than 5 percent of the capital available.

Shareholders can determine a risk-reward ratio as well. A chance-reward rate can be 1:3 if an investor theoretically has a limit of $300 to lose and a maximum of $600 for investment advantage.

Please note that risk management is critical, especially in this volatile stock market. Investing requires an evaluation of one's risk tolerance, and this risk tolerance is never tested more than amid a bear market."

Traders might fear to miss what they can spare. Establishing a stop loss will help investors stay with their investment limits, particularly in forex. A stop-order loss is an allot to sell a capital once a specific price has been reached. Investors can limit their exposure to the risk by setting a stop-loss.

For instance, at 1.1233, a trader could be trading the euro and the dollar. The trader could pledge to sell the EUR / USD if it dropped below 1.12. A stop-loss will reduce the amount an investor loses on a deal.

I noted that the best way to minimise risk is by stop-loss orders. I have a predetermined stop [loss] whenever I step into a position. All I can do is sleep that way. I know where I am going to get out before I get in. The size of the area on a trade determined by the stop [loss] and the stop is determined technically. I always put my stop beyond some technical barrier, "it is essential to research in addition to setting limits on investment."

No, the newspaper isn't thinking about crushes. A daily business journal can help an investor keep track of how the trades are going and how your overall plan is doing. A trading journal helps an investor keep track of what works and what doesn't work in a trading strategy. These main aspects should apply to trade journals.

Date and Trading Time. Could you keep track of when they made trades? Investors may find deals done in the morning more beneficial than businesses at different times.

Trace different tools. An investor may own capital in various instruments, such as commodities and stocks. Investors can watch each particular instrument's output to decide how their trading strategy works for each investment. Prizes for entrance and departure. When entering and exiting trades, an investor should keep track of stock prices. Trades results. Study business results. Investors will then carry on successes and mistakes.

When a trading journal is checked, an investor may notice a pattern in a trading plan, especially when there are losses. To perfect its trading strategy, an investor must learn from mistakes. Believes that failures are a natural part of trade and that investors can learn from omissions and errors in trading.

"I don't think you can be a winning trader consistently if you're banking more than 50 percent of the time right. You have to work out how to make money just 20 to 30 percent of the time."

For example, poor risk management, which uses too much leverage and an adverse risk/reward profile on trades, is a staple of poor risk management. I find (as a rule of thumb, a trader should not engage in business unless analysis suggests that they can make at least ~$2 for every $1 that is risky).

Knowledge of information regarding trading is essential. Noted, however, the over-analysis may also delay traders. "The analytical process is overcomplicated.

Often traders using too much knowledge to make conclusions resulting in inconsistency and indecisive behaviour, through their trading tactics, a trader will know what worked and what didn't work.

Even if a trading strategy hasn't worked, they may learn to continue as a trader from their mistakes. Investors should either tweak their plans or seek out a brand new one, and losses should not deter traders. They should re-evaluate their strategy and remain in the investment game. Investors will be motivated by being optimistic and viewing investing as a severe company. Investors should use several different trading approaches to develop their profitable trading strategy to become a good trader.

5.4 Be Very Cautious with Leverage

Leverage means investing any of the capital needed to invest in it. In the forex case, a broker usually borrows money. Forex trading offers a tremendous advantage where a trader can build and control an immense amount of money for an initial margin requirement.

Is your online trading platform allowing you to use the leverage when doing business? If so, you can trade in just $100 of capital for $3,000.

If you end up with a deficit, you have spent more money on your bankroll than you have. Being very cautious about leveraging is critical, as you can also incur severe losses.

Keep the experts on leverage trading, or at least don't start your trading activities with leverage until you have the best grasp of what works and what doesn't.

E.g., if you expected to deposit 1 percent of the overall value of the deal as a margin and plan to exchange one regular batch of USD / CHF equal to US$ 100,000, the margin expected will be US$ 1000. So, your leverage based on the margins will be 100:1 (100,000/1,000). The margin-based advantage would be 400:1, using the same calculation, with a margin allowance of just 0.25 percent.

Margin-Based Leverage Expressed as Ratio	Margin Required of Total Transaction Value
400:1	0.25%
200:1	0.50%
100:1	1.00%
50:1	2.00%

Nonetheless, margin-based leverage does not automatically impact risk and whether an investor forced to offer up 1 percent or 2 percent of the deal's value as margin does not change their gains or losses. This is because, for any position, the investor can always attribute more than the required margin. It indicates that the real leverage is the more definite indicator of profit and loss, not a margin-based advantage.

For instance, if you have $10,000 in your statement and you open a $100,000 position similar to one standard lot, you'll be trading on your account with ten times the leverage (100,000/10,000). If you purchase two standard lots with a face value of $200,000 with $10,000 in your account, your account leverage is twenty times (200,000/10,000).

It also means that the leverage depending on the spreads is equal to the maximum real force that an investor can use. Since most traders use none of their balances as spreads on all of their trades, their net profit remains unchanged over their margin-based leverages.

A trader shouldn't generally use all of their available margins. A dealer cannot use the leverage while there is a definite advantage on their hand. When the amount of exposure known about the number of pips, the estimated capital loss will calculate.

As a rule, this loss should never amount to more than 3 percent of trading stock. If a position is to strengthen to the point that, say, 30 percent of trading capital could be the potential loss, this measure should reduce the leverage. Traders may have their level of expertise and risk thresholds and should opt to deviate from the 3 percent general guideline.

Also, traders will measure the margin rates they should be using. Suppose you have 10,000 dollars in your brokerage account, and you plan to exchange ten mini lots of USD / JPY. Each move of one pip in a small statement is worth about $1, but each pip move is worth around $10 when trading ten minis. When you transact 100 minis, per pip transfer is worth about $100. A stop-loss of 30 pips could thus represent a potential loss of $30 for one mini lot, $300 for ten small lots, and $3,000 for 100 mini lots. Therefore, you should only maximise up to 30 mini lots with a $10,000 account and a 3 percent average cost per deal, even though you may have the ability to trade more.

The leverage is commonly as high as 100:1 in the foreign exchange markets. That means you can exchange up to $ 100,000 in interest for every $1,000 you have in your account. Many traders believe that the reason Forex market makers are offering such high leverage is that leverage is a risk function. We know that if the loan is managed correctly, the burden would also be very manageable, or they would not be providing flexibility.

And, since the spot cash forex markets are so big and flexible, it's much easier to enter and exit a transaction at the desired price than in other less liquid markets.

We monitor currency movements in pips in trading, which is the slightest change in currency price and depends on the currency pair. Such motions are, in general, just fractions of one cent.

For example, when a currency pair such as the GBP / USD changes 100 pips from 1.9500 to 1.9600 — that is, the exchange rate changes is only 1 cent.

This is why currency trades have to be carried out in substantial quantities, enabling such minute market fluctuations to be converted into more significant gains when magnified by leveraging use. When you handle an amount like $100,000, small changes in the currency's price can result in substantial profits or losses.

This is where the double-fringe sword comes in, as the original purchase has the potential to increase the same magnitude of your profits or losses. The higher the amount of leverage you apply on the capital, the higher the risk you'll assume. Notice that this risk is not necessarily related to margin-based advantage, although if a trader is not cautious, it can affect it.

Let's take an example to highlight this point. Trader A and Trader B both have a US$ 10,000 trading capital and trade with a broker that requires a margin deposit of 1 percent. After some analysis, both agree that USD / JPY is hitting a top and should fall in value. Hence, both are shortening the USD / JPY at 120.

Trader A decides to add actual leverage 50 times to this deal by shortening US$ 500,000 worth of dollar / JPY (50 x $10,000) build on their trading capital of $10,000. Since USD / JPY is 120, one pip of USD / JPY for one standard lot is worth about US$ 8.30, meaning that one pip of USD / JPY for five standard lots is worth about US$ 41.50. If USD / JPY falls to 121, Trader A on this contract will lose 100 tanks, which is similar to a loss of US$ 4,150. This single loss would account for a whopping 41.5 percent of their entire market income.

Investor B is a more cautious investor and wants to add actual leverage five times to this deal by shortening US$ 50,000 worth of USD / JPY (5 x $10,000) based on their market capital of $10,000. That $50,000 worth of USD / JPY is a mere half of a standard lot. If dollar / JPY rises to 121, Trader B will mislay 100 pips on this trade, equivalent to a $415 loss. This one loss accounts for 4.15 percent of their entire market value.

There's no reason to doubt power until you've learned how to use it. The only time you should never use the leverage is to take a hands-off approach to your trades. Otherwise, the advantage of proper management can be used successfully and profitably.

Like any sharp instrument, the force has to be handled carefully — once you've learned to do this, there's no reason to worry.

Little amounts of real leverage applied to each trade provide more breathing space by putting a more complete but reasonable stop and avoiding more significant capital loss. If it goes against you, a highly leveraged business can quickly deplete your trading account, as you will rack up more considerable losses due to the larger lot sizes. Bear in mind that the leverage is entirely adjustable and can tailor to each trader's needs.

5.5 Don't Become Emotionally Attached

Based on your work, you made a deal. You're sure there's going to be a currency going up, but you're getting close to a loss. It's time to get out of the trade, but several traders get emotionally addicted and never really leave the company.

It puts you at the chance of losing money if you become emotionally attached to any investments.

Traders directly attached to market act with a process-oriented attitude and do not judge their skill or system by the result of a deal but on how he takes his judgment.

It is crucial to understand that you will always experience emotions to some extent and that you cannot avoid feelings, but do not make impulsive trade decisions. Even under pressure or when dealing with a position against you, you can evaluate the situation objectively and make rational trade decisions based on your business plan. However, most traders regularly experience trade attachment, which causes them to lose money even though it might have been kept away or at least limited. The difference between an amateur and a professional trader is not that the expert is not losing trades – he is missing all the time – but knows how to lose correctly and move on.

Leave feelings behind, and instead of using commerce as an opportunity when an investment starts to lose money or makes no sense anymore, exit.

Trading with emotional commitment would deter you from making the best choices to make money and protect your property. Emotions impair your judgment and don't encourage you to interpret market facts critically. Emotional commitment to stocks means you are not buying and selling at the right times.

Traders who become emotionally attached to stocks that they own often turn into bag holders, as their emotions keep them from respecting price action. Here are three explanations why, and how to stop, traders develop an emotional attachment to their stocks.

Oversized trading with too much size is the most common cause of the traders' emotional attachment. They trade with capital, which they cannot afford to lose. When you deal with a lot of your net worth, you'll put a lot of feelings into your trading. In a transaction where you gamble the money you need to pay your deposit, you'll be very emotional. You should never risk money, which will make you change your lifestyle.

Contrary to what new traders may assume, the decreasing size would make you money from your company. You worry less about the money when your size decreases, and as a result, you deal with a less emotional attachment to the stock you have on the market. You will be able to make trade decisions based on your plan when you have a less emotional attachment to the money.

Focused on cash and not even on the market, traders who don't risk huge suffer from emotional attachment because they don't want to lose money.

They are so attached to the cash that they panic whenever the market goes a bit against them, and they are temporarily down on money. As a result, they can never hold a winning position long enough because each time the market makes an unavoidable move against their job, they panic sell or cover it. They are upset about the money they have on the market, rather than the signals that the market tells you.

No stock goes directly upwards or downwards. A market shifting against your position doesn't mean that your trade theory is false. In the stock exchange, you never make $1000 without losing at least $500 of the money you spend. Unless you gamble capital, you will become a good trader — the inevitability of losing trades.

Once you establish and execute a profitable trading strategy, in the long run, you will be making money. Losing trades is only the price you pay to make a living on the stock market. Remember that if you're in a business and you're going to get afraid of wasting the money you've got on the market, it will remind you not to become emotionally attached to the money that you risk and let the trade play out.

Successful traders do business with the ticker, not the company. Losing traders fell in love with the CEO, the result of the firms, their team, etc.

As a consequence, they stop respecting price action, and hold on to a losing trade because they are attached to the company. They believe the so-called "good fundamentals" are an excuse for holding on to a position on which they are down 40 percent.

Active investing is the product of market action valued, not that you are buying the firms you want. Just because you love the mattresses of Sears doesn't mean that you can buy the collection. You will risk a lot of money if you do because they go bankrupt.

The reverse scenario is shorting a company that you don't like. Small-cap stocks are quite familiar to this. Losing traders are short just because a junk company is 100% up, and they think it will be 0. It then goes up by 200 percent, and the money of the merchants is gone.

Never become emotionally attached to the firms you buy or are short. On the phone, they are all clearly maps. When you press the buy and sale keys, do not let your emotional commitment to the client decide.

Although it is crucial to have self-esteem and confidence in your system, letting your ego get in the way while making trade decisions is fatal. Reflect on process-oriented thinking, work on your due diligence, and be prepared for any eventualities as we have mentioned before.

Even then, don't judge your skills based on a trade result, and consider long-term. In a life of a trader, one trade does not mean anything.

It's a nasty habit to continually watch your P&L go up and down with every price tick that has a significant impact on how you make your trade decisions. When you see that price in a winning trade is going against you and that your P&L is going low, you are more likely to end a deal too early, although there are no clear signals of exit.

Reflect more on the maps, and on what you may find critically. Review your trading strategy often to create faith and confidence and prevent impulsive trading decisions.

5.6 Learn All About Risk Management

It's time to continue if you haven't learned about risk management. Each trade has its inherent risks, so it is up to you to do good, risk-taking trades.

To preserve what you have, you need to try it out. Profits come second, as you risk the opportunity to make some income if the money washed out.

One method of managing the risk is to place stop-loss orders. Lot sizes should be appropriate and should know when to leave a market.

Risk management is one of the significant critical facets of active trading. The task of a trader is to keep you in the market at all times. A good plan and the follow-up consistency will go a long way to ensuring that you stick with it.

When you're in the learning stage, you aim to keep losses very low before you figure out what you are doing from an objective and theoretical point of view. Adhering to sound risk thresholds early on would go a long way towards later developing a base.

You aim to avoid digging needless holes for the more experienced dealer, and of course, avoid the possibility of disaster. You may have a workable strategy, but maybe you are applying inconsistent risk management rules that might affect your ability to grow.

Talk about the amount of money you want to lose, not how many points or pipes you want. When you take this approach, your trading size will be dynamic. Let's assume you lose 1 percent of trade; the scale of the transaction would be twice as high on a 50 pip stop trading as opposed to trading where the stop is 100 pips away. In this scenario, if you keep the trade size stable, the probability would stay the same.

However, if you think in terms of set lot sizes, the chance will change with time, and so will the outcomes.

Let's assume, for example, that you have an average win/loss ratio of 1:2. If you gamble 50 pips on trading # 1 and make 100 pips (2x chance), you'll be 100 pips. So, you risk 100 pips on trading, and it reaches your exit, you'll lose 100 pips. If you trade in total lots sizes, this will result in a net of 0 between the two trades.

However, you'll get a competitive result by taking a balanced strategy and changing your trading size to suit your percentage per trade-risk. Let's presume you gamble 1% on trading # 1 and make 2%, then gamble 1% on trading # 2 and loose, you're only going to come out +1%. It's a simple example, but it should be clear on principle.

You want the risk-per-trade to be accurate. For one proposal, you don't want to gamble for 0.5 percent, 3 percent for the next one, then 1 percent after that, and so on. As if using set lot sizes, the findings are going to be all over the world. Perhaps you're incredibly optimistic about an idea and want to gamble a bit more than average, that's cool as long as it doesn't change too much from your standard scale of trading. High systems usually don't have as much variation in the probability of performance from one to the next, as you would expect.

The primary goal should be to find trades that provide an edge and an asymmetric risk profile. Risk/reward can or should be around 1:2 or equivalent. So many traders get caught up on a high probability of winning, which is understandable to some degree – people don't like losing, so that's part of the game. Better having a win rate of 30 percent with a 1:5 R/R ratio, than a win rate of 60 percent with a 1:1 R/R ratio.

Account Risk management is just one element of a good plan. You also need to protect the total account by considering a few factors. Setting stop-loss and take-profit points is mostly achieved using quantitative analysis, but a crucial role in timing can often play by fundamental analysis.

If a trader keeps a stock ahead of earnings as anticipation rises, he or she will decide to sell before the news hits the market as expectations have become too high, regardless of whether the profit-taking price has hit.

The most common way to set these points is by moving averages since they are easy to measure and commonly followed by the market. Ideally, these are determined by adding them to a stock chart and evaluating how the stock price responded to either a degree of support or resistance.

Another perfect way to put stop-loss or take-profit rates is on-trend lines of encouragement or opposition.

It can derive by comparing previous peaks or lows that happened at a considerable amount above normal. The aim is to decide the rate at which the price will respond to the trend lines like with moving averages and, of course, the high volume.

Here are few primary factors when setting such points: using longer-term trading averages to reduce the risk of a pointless price change causing a stop-loss order to execute.

The moving averages calibrated to match target price ranges. More extended targets, such as more excellent moving averages, reduce the number of generated signals.

Stop losses will not be the present high-to-low level (volatility) higher than 1.5-times, because it is more likely to be performed without justification. Change the stop loss depending on the size of the market when the stock price doesn't drop too far, reinforcing the stop-loss points.

They were using established simple events such as earnings reports, as first-time intervals will grow to be in or out of business as instability and confusion.

Traders will also learn, before conducting, whether they intend to join or leave a deal. When actively using stop losses, a trader can reduce not only damages but also needlessly the amount of times a transaction exited.

In conclusion, make your battle plan ahead of time, so you'll know that you've already won the war. This is how we can learn about risk management and be a successful trader.

Conclusion

So, what is options trading? It is the process of buying and selling put and call options. It may include simple strategies such as long calls or put-ins. But, remember, options trading is not appropriate for every investor. Besides, be aware of transaction costs, especially when dealing with strategies that involve more than one contract, which can have a notable impact on any potential gain or loss.

A deep-in-money call strategy is the best way to acquire stocks artificially, but more than half the money is at risk. Do other technologies give you so much return on your capital and allow you to take the same action? I don't know anyone, that's why I use Ditm trading. Stay with Leaps options that will enable you to control the stock for up to three years and allow you to invest money in the income securities you offer. Take advantage of the delta factor using options with at least 90 percent delta. The put-sale strategy not only gives you revenue from the buyer, but it also allows you to buy low-quality stock.

The credit spread option allows you to take your directional calls and get a large margin for error.

Even if the market can go against you, the chances are that option strikes are out of money. These are the singles and doubles you are targeting. There are no fences here because most of them are trade hits. Covered Call is another excellent option-selling technique that allows you to earn cash flow every few months of the year. Since you have the stock, who would have thought that someone would give you money? It is an excellent concept if you know how to use it. Remember, stick to money-laundering options to reduce your recruiting opportunities. Finally, spread selection is one of the riskiest choices, and the most attractive options trading strategy yet. Be sharp, and stay on your toes with it. It has unlimited risk potential, so you want to consider anything before starting this business seriously. Although the risks are high, the profit potential is beautiful. Make sure you use options outside of the money for both legs of the spread, and the distance between strikes is vast.

The binary options strategy requires a calm head and a lot of planning for a successful business. The market tests your will power and subjectivity, so stick to your binary options strategy no matter what your initial trades' results are.

Remember, no strategy is 100% successful. Knowledge is your great ally in this business, so study everything before making your first investment.

Demo accounts are advantageous when they allow you to see what a particular fund is offering without risking any of your funds. Also, they are often entirely independent and, therefore, should be an indispensable tool in their preparation as most brokers offer one of these.

Preparation, planning, and persistence is an essential requirement for profit in this business. This book has a lot of information, all of which are options to help you better prepare for trading stocks and use technical analysis in particular. Trading is action, and like any other process, the more you make and the more you practice, the better you are set up for a good start. Understanding the trend "started this process. We have figured out how to identify the main trend and what its impact is. It is important because 70% or more of all stocks are in trend. Then we market the found areas in a layer of onion structure. With only two processes to master, "How is the market moving, and how can I use that information?" By answering the question, you are ready to make the most significant decisions in your investment and business life. Do you dare? "